KNITTING
FOR YOUR HOME

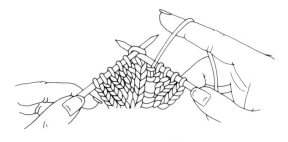

Rita Weiss

Photographs by
Stanley A. Lomas

Drawings by
Frank Fontana

 Van Nostrand Reinhold Company
New York Cincinnati Toronto London Melbourne

Acknowledgments

The following group of devoted friends tested the instructions in this book by making the articles that were photographed:

Janice Anderson	Joy Elliott	Stephanie Sipp
Barbara Brondolo	Ida Jablon	Betty Telford
Libby Doof	Ruth Keats	Michelle Weiss
Adele Durkin	Bella Moltz	Sabrina Weiss
Frances Durkin	Ruth Myer	

I should also like to thank the following companies who were kind enough to supply yarn used to make some of these projects:

American Thread Company   DMC Corporation   Lily Mills Company

FOR JACK
Who indulges my whims

Book design by Carol Belanger Grafton

Published by Van Nostrand Reinhold Company
A division of Litton Educational Publishing, Inc.
135 West 50th Street, New York, NY 10020, U.S.A.

Van Nostrand Reinhold Limited
1410 Birchmount Road, Scarborough, Ontario M1P 2E7, Canada

Van Nostrand Reinhold Australia Pty. Ltd.
17 Queen Street, Mitcham, Victoria 3132, Australia

Van Nostrand Reinhold Company Limited
Molly Millars Lane, Wokingham, Berkshire, England

16 15 14 13 12 11 10 9 8 7 6 5 4 3 2 1

Library of Congress Cataloging in Publication Data

Weiss, Rita.
    Knitting for your home.
    Includes index.
    1. Knitting. I. Title.
TT820.W358   746.4'32   79-22537
ISBN 0-442-24335-9

CONTENTS

INTRODUCTION

I was introduced to the joy of knitting as a little girl in elementary school during the Second World War. My teacher, Miss Marx, gathered a group of eager little girls (those were sexist times; knitting was not the province of men) and taught us to knit so that we could aid the war effort. Our task was to knit colorful squares, which she then joined together into huge afghans for the Red Cross.

I never quite ascertained how the Red Cross made use of the afghans; we were told that they were used in hospitals to cover wounded soldiers. For some childish reason I felt that the faster I knitted, the sooner the war would be over. I have secretly believed, all these years, that I single-handedly defeated Hitler with my knitting needles.

I loved knitting those squares. There were no instructions to be slavishly followed or knitting shorthand to be learned. You merely knitted a square approximately 6'' x 6''. It didn't matter if the square ended up being 6 3/4'' x 6 1/2''. Somehow the squares all fitted together into a gigantic, colorful afghan. We had our pictures taken holding the finished project, the huge smiles on our faces attesting to the joy of knitting. Then off the afghans went with our love to the "who knows where" corners of the world.

My afghan knitting days ended with the conclusion of the war, but I went on to knit bigger and more imposing projects. Knitting is habit forming, and once you have become accustomed to working with your needles while listening to the radio, traveling in buses or trains, talking to friends, or even reading the newspaper, you will find it difficult to involve yourself in these activities without first putting needles into your hands. Since there were no longer any battles to win with knitted afghans, I took to making other projects. What I was knitting at the time seemed to parallel the periods of my own life. I ran through the period of argyle socks. (You knitted those down to the toe, and then you waited for the appropriate young man to come along, at which time you measured his feet and hurriedly completed the socks for his birthday or for Valentine's Day. He was terribly impressed with your ability as a knitter since he assumed that you had knitted the socks overnight. According to all of the women's magazines of the era, this was supposed to lead to an immediate proposal of marriage. What a great little housewife you would make!) My young husband had to

be measured for a sweater on our honeymoon, and as soon as the rabbit gave me the word, I began to knit little baby sacques in pale shades of yellow, green, pink and blue. Later I knitted mittens by the acre, and made hats, scarves and sweaters in varying sizes for growing children.

But the joy of knitting never quite equaled those square-knitting days in Miss Marx's classroom. I soon discovered that in order to follow knitting instructions you had to learn how to knit to a gauge and to understand the knitter's "shorthand." No matter how hard I tried, I could never get my gauge to equal the gauge in the instructions. I'd do all of the things the instruction writer would suggest: try larger needles, try smaller needles, cast on more stitches, cast on fewer stitches. Inevitably, a size 34 sweater ended up fitting either a size 40 or a size 32.

The knitting shorthand also took much of the joy out of knitting. It was bad enough to have to remember what the "psso's" and the "yo's" were supposed to mean, when suddenly, while I'd be knitting along at a great clip a "K1b" or a "wfd" would appear. Then, while holding my place in the instructions, I'd have to flip to the front of the book to find the list of "translations." The joy of accomplishment was sometimes worth the effort, but there is a trunk in my basement filled with projects that were never completed because the "sl1's" and the "p4's" got hopelessly confused with the "yo's" and the "psso's."

I loved to knit for others, especially for my husband and daughters. This knitting for others, however, is what almost completely destroyed my desire to knit. The mittens I had spent three television programs doing disappeared one at a time into a mysterious snowdrift. The sweaters I had worked on until my shoulders ached were often rolled up and used for pillows while their teen-age owners read their latest homework assignments. How many times did I catch a young cook using a scarf or even the sleeve of a hand-knitted sweater as a pot holder! The most crushing blow, the straw that broke the knitter's stitch, came the day that one of my daughters carried home a plant in her knitted hat, unmindful that the potting soil had worked its way into the tightly knitted stitches. I swore I would never knit again!

But once a knitter, always a knitter. I tired of other crafts—including needlepoint and embroidery—because I never quite experienced the satisfaction that I had from knitting. Finally I decided that if I couldn't defeat the world I would join it. Since my family preferred to roll up their sweaters and put them under their heads, I'd make knitted pillows. Since scarves and sleeves were used for pot holders, why not knit pot holders? And the plant carried home in the hat gave me the idea for knitted plant holders. I would invent simple patterns. I would return to those joyful days in Miss Marx's class, and I'd knit square after square, which could then be turned into something beautiful and useful.

And so began a new era of knitting. Not for fickle boyfriends who didn't see the quick knitting of argyle socks as a criterion for selecting a wife; not for husbands who didn't like wearing sweaters in which one arm didn't quite match the other; not for little babies who spit up all over carefully knitted sacques; not for little girls who lost their mittens; not for teenagers who turned beautifully knitted sweaters into pillows; but *for my home,* which accepts all my projects with no apparent disdain. I still spend a great deal of my spare time knitting because I now know that the finished project will remain as long as it continues to bring *me* pleasure.

In this book I will share with you some of my favorite projects. I assume that you know how to knit and purl, but that, like me, you want to knit new and different projects that will be fun to knit. If you have forgotten what you once learned about knitting and purling, casting on and off, knitting with two colors, or any of the other basics of knitting—or if you have never learned and want to start now—I've explained it to you in the appendix.

Absent from this book are some of the more frustrating elements found in most knitting books. I have simplified the instructions by completely eliminating the knitting shorthand. I will never tell you to "yo" or "sl1." Instead I will ask you to "yarn over" or "slip 1." If it is necessary to decrease or increase, I will tell you how to do it by asking you to "knit 2 together" or "knit in the front and the back of the stitch." I have used two symbols which are traditionally used in knitting patterns: a pair of asterisks (*) and a set of parentheses ( ). The asterisks (*) mean that you should keep repeating the directions inside the asterisks as indicated in the instructions. "Repeat from * to * across the row" means that you should repeat the directions within the asterisks over and over again across the row until the entire row is completed. A set of parentheses ( ) means that you should work the directions

within the parentheses ( ) the number of times indicated in the directions and then continue to work the rest of the row or the round.

Knitting to the correct gauge will be of little importance in this book. There are a few projects that will require a gauge, but it really won't matter if your gauge is larger or smaller since no one will ever wear any of these projects. Your house won't mind if an afghan ends up being larger or smaller than an afghan made by your dear Aunt Tillie. I have also tried to eliminate the dependence upon crocheting that most knitting books seem to share. I've given you instructions for making knitted edgings rather than asking you to crochet edges. In several of the projects I've indicated a crocheted trim as an optional device because I know that many knitters like this effect. If you are not a crocheter, you can still complete any of these projects.

I've tried to make all of the projects the kind that can be completed in a few hours or a few days rather than the kind that become lifelong undertakings. I would have liked to have included a knitted bedspread and a huge, elaborate lace tablecloth, but I know such projects can be terribly time-consuming and discouraging. I have substituted a patchwork quilt and a simple lace tablecloth. Both of these projects are easy to make and work up very quickly.

Many of the projects call for the use of a circular needle because I love working with one. If you have never used a circular needle, you are missing one of the great joys of knitting. You do have to begin by knitting on four needles until you have enough stitches—about 40-50—on your needles to be able to transfer onto the circular needle. In the beginning you may find the four-needle stage a bit clumsy, but with a little experience, you will enjoy working with a circular needle. In fact, I often use a circular needle to knit in rows, working back and forth rather than in rounds. Stitches can't fall off a circular needle, and you can't suddenly lose one of the needles in the middle of a project.

In many ways this book asks you to forget many of the rules you have learned about knitting. I've tried to return knitting to that simple joyous craft I experienced in Miss Marx's class. In most of the projects you just knit, and when you feel that your piece is the correct size, you stop. Forget the preconceived ideas you may have about knitting. Forget most of the old rules; the only rule you have to follow now is to have fun knitting.

1.

THE LIVING ROOM

When I was a young girl the family living room—or front room as it was called—was used only for very special occasions such as entertaining very elegant guests like my brother's fourth-grade teacher, who came to announce that my brother was a veritable genius. The white sheets that covered the furniture were only removed for those extraordinary moments when the living room was opened. On those special holidays we wore our best clothes and sat upright on the living room chairs, not daring to breathe for fear that we might crush the crushed velvet upholstery.

Once a week someone—and it usually was the only daughter in the household—was given a dust cloth and sent into the room to carefully dust the unused furniture. In the winter the heat was turned off in the unused rooms. The lack of heat was not just an attempt to save money. We heated with coal in those days, and so a thin film of dirt covered everything. If you kept the heat registers closed, the curtains stayed white and the wallpaper persevered for a few more years. I learned how to dust wearing a heavy coat, exhaling huge clouds of icy air as I trudged through the room.

No family member or close friend ever used the front door because that would necessitate walking through the living room. All deliveries had to be made through the kitchen door, and even the family doctor—who naïvely made house calls—came through the kitchen door with his worn bag replete with healing devices. Occasionally some unsuspecting individual would ring the front doorbell, completely upsetting my mother, who would have frightening visions of bearlike dirty footprints appearing on her oriental carpet.

The advent of television introduced a degree of sanity into our house by acquainting us with that long-neglected shrine, our living room. The arrival of a television set in our household was a grand occasion of the type that was worthy of opening the living room. Decorating magazines had been caught off guard, and hadn't yet taught us that special rooms should be set aside for TV viewing. Television viewing encourages slovenly habits. There are the commercials that send you to the refrigerator for a snack to provide enough nourishment to endure the next segment. We no longer sat upright in our chairs because television is almost hypnotic, leading to everyone's watching it in a supine position on the couch or slung over the sides of a chair.

Despite my mother's valiant efforts to keep the furniture covered, the sheets would end up on the floor long before the evening was over, and someone's dirty shoes would inevitably make their mark on the upholstery, coffee cake crumbs would be ground into the crevices of the couch, or coffee would be spilled on the table (which I had spent my girlhood carefully polishing every Saturday morning). Within a few years the living room had been reduced to the stature of a barn.

The decorating gurus, however, soon caught onto the disaster that was being perpetrated upon living rooms throughout the country. By the time I was decorating my own home, we were enjoined to have a family room or den in our households for the hard living that went with TV viewing, and the living room was returned to its pre-TV status, reserved for special occasions. We could now fill our living rooms with the elegant furniture it deserved.

Plastic slipcovers replaced my mother's old sheets, and the front door was moved so that you didn't have to walk through the living room to answer the front doorbell. The once-a-week dusting became easier, too, because we stopped heating with coal, and we now had air-conditioners, which removed most of the dust from the rooms. Special finishes on the furniture and new waxes made polishing a simple chore not a childhood disease.

I happen to like to sit in my own living room, but, in a way, I am pleased that most of my family prefers sitting in less elegant parts of the house, where they don't have to be worried about disturbing their mother if they should spill something on the wall-to-wall carpet. I like to sit quietly reading or just thinking in a room that is furnished as beautifully as I desire but has no maintenance problems to concern me.

You are going to find some very old-fashioned things in this chapter because I like to think of today's formal living room in the same terms as those nostalgic memories of the "front room" I so revered as a child. Since the heat in my living room is turned down just as it was in my mother's living room (we're more concerned about the energy crisis than about the coal dust that bothered my mother) I've included instructions for an afghan and what I call a "warm-all."

If your own mode of living doesn't include two living areas, you may want to turn to the section on knitting for the family room or den, which contains more ideas for informal living.

MISS MARX'S AFGHAN DONE ONE BETTER

What could be more elegant when casually flung over a couch than a beautiful afghan made in colors to match or coordinate with the colors in your room? Even if the afghan is never used, it adds lovely color to the room. If you like to sit in your living room, there's nothing more comfortable or cozy than sitting under a lovely afghan.

This afghan is actually an adaptation of the afghans we knitted for Miss Marx—the project that first "hooked" me on knitting. The afghan is actually made up of twenty-four 11″ (28cm) squares. You can, if you wish, knit twenty-four individual squares and then join them to make the afghan. I prefer to knit the squares in four long strips, each containing six squares, and then to join the strips together. The long strips are not as portable as the individual squares might be, but I find it easier to do it this way because then I only have to make three seams rather than twenty-three.

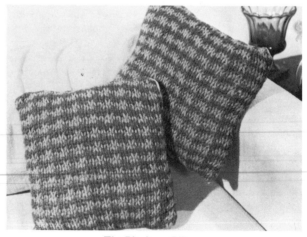

The Blocks as Pillows

I've added another twist to Miss Marx's original afghan: each square is made in a different stitch. When you have completed this afghan, you'll have learned to do twenty-four knitting stitches or patterns, and you can actually use this as a sampler for future knitting. If you like a particular stitch, you might try to use it for another project in this or any other knitting book.

In the center of the afghan there are eight blocks which are made with bicolor stitches. These stitches are made with a slip-and-knit technique. Do not carry the color not in use across the row; leave it at the side to be picked up on the return row. Many of these stitches, by the way, make interesting and different patterns on the reverse side. When you are looking for new stitches, reverse your afghan and look at the back.

You will occasionally be asked to add or subtract a stitch. This should make no difference in the final size of your block. Complex stitches must be done in specific multiples, and in order to achieve the pattern it will be necessary to have a certain number of stitches on the needle. Some of the stitches will distort your knitting but with careful blocking they can be straightened. Don't be dismayed, therefore, if you discover that one block is moving off on the diagonal. You will be able to straighten it.

You don't really have to worry about gauge in this project. If your particular knitting is making the block wider or narrower than the suggested 11″, just change the length of each block accordingly so that each block is a square.

You can choose one or two stitch patterns that you particularly like and do the entire afghan in those stitches, switching colors every 11″ (28cm). You can also make the afghan in a multitude of colors, using up scraps of yarn that you have available. Each square can be a different color and a different stitch.

Done individually, the blocks will make great throw pillows to match your afghan. Just knit two blocks according to the instructions. Join the two blocks, leaving the top open. Stuff with polyester fiberfill or foam rubber cut to size. Close the opening.

Since this afghan is going to teach you how to do a number of different stitches, a picture of how each stitch will look when it is completed appears above the instructions for that particular block.

SIZE: Approximately 44″ x 66″ (112cm x 167.5cm).

MATERIALS: 24 ounces aqua four-ply knitting worsted, 24 ounces royal blue four-ply knitting worsted, size 7 knitting needles, cable holder or double-pointed knitting needle, size G crochet hook (optional).

FIRST STRIP

Moss Stitch

Block One: Moss Stitch

DIRECTIONS: With royal blue, cast on 58 stitches.
Row 1: *Knit 1, purl 1.* Repeat from * to * across the row.
Row 2: *Purl 1, knit 1.* Repeat from * to * across the row.
Repeat these 2 rows until the square measures 11″ (28cm).

Garter Stitch

Block Two: Garter Stitch

DIRECTIONS: Cut royal blue and attach aqua.
Row 1: Knit.
Row 2: Knit.
Repeat these 2 rows until the square measures 11″ (28cm).

Stockinette Stitch

Block Three: Stockinette Stitch

DIRECTIONS: Cut aqua and attach royal blue.
Row 1: Knit.
Row 2: Purl.
Repeat these 2 rows until the square measures 11″ (28cm).

Reverse Stockinette Stitch

Block Four: Reverse Stockinette Stitch

DIRECTIONS: Cut royal blue and attach aqua.
Row 1: Purl.
Row 2: Knit.
Repeat these 2 rows until the square measures 11″ (28cm).
This stitch is just what the name implies: the reverse of the stich used in Block Three.

Ridged Rib Stitch

Block Five: Ridged Rib Stitch

DIRECTIONS: Cut aqua and attach royal blue.

Row 1: Knit.	**Row 7:** Purl.
Row 2: Purl.	**Row 8:** Knit.
Row 3: Knit.	**Row 9:** Purl.
Row 4: Purl.	**Row 10:** Knit.
Row 5: Knit.	**Row 11:** Purl.
Row 6: Purl.	**Row 12:** Knit.

Repeat these 12 rows until the square measures 11″ (28cm). In the sample afghan, these 12 rows were repeated 5 times and the block completed with rows 1–6.

Basket-Weave Stitch

Block Six: Basket-Weave Stitch

DIRECTIONS: Cut royal blue and attach aqua.
Row 1: Knit 8, (purl 6, knit 6) 3 times, purl 6, knit 8.
Row 2: Purl 8, (knit 6, purl 6) 3 times, knit 6, purl 8.
Rows 3, 5, and 7: Repeat row 1.
Rows 4 and 6: Repeat row 2.
Repeat these 7 rows until the square measures 11″ (28cm). In the sample afghan, these 7 rows were repeated 10 times.
Bind off the strip.

SECOND STRIP

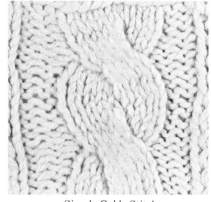

Simple Cable Stitch

Block One: Simple Cable Stitch

DIRECTIONS: With aqua, cast on 58 stitches.
Rows 1, 3 and 5: Knit 4, purl 3, knit 8, purl 3, knit 22, purl 3, knit 8, purl 3, knit 4.
Rows 2, 4 and 6: Purl 4, knit 3, purl 8, knit 3, purl 22, knit 3, purl 8, knit 3, purl 4.
Row 7: Knit 4, purl 3, slip the next 4 stitches onto a cable holder or double-pointed needle and leave at the front of the work, knit 4, knit the 4 stitches from the cable holder or double-pointed needle, purl 3, knit 22, purl 3, slip the next 4 stitches onto a cable holder or double-pointed needle and leave at the front of the work, knit 4, knit the 4 stitches from the cable holder or double-pointed needle, purl 3, knit 4.
Row 8: Repeat row 2.
Repeat these 8 rows until the square measures 11″ (28cm).

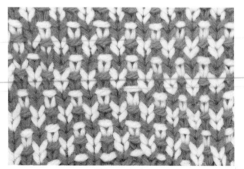

Woven Stitch

I've added another twist to Miss Marx's original afghan: each square is made in a different stitch. When you have completed this afghan, you'll have learned to do twenty-four knitting stitches or patterns, and you can actually use this as a sampler for future knitting. If you like a particular stitch, you might try to use it for another project in this or any other knitting book.

In the center of the afghan there are eight blocks which are made with bicolor stitches. These stitches are made with a slip-and-knit technique. Do not carry the color not in use across the row; leave it at the side to be picked up on the return row. Many of these stitches, by the way, make interesting and different patterns on the reverse side. When you are looking for new stitches, reverse your afghan and look at the back.

You will occasionally be asked to add or subtract a stitch. This should make no difference in the final size of your block. Complex stitches must be done in specific multiples, and in order to achieve the pattern it will be necessary to have a certain number of stitches on the needle. Some of the stitches will distort your knitting but with careful blocking they can be straightened. Don't be dismayed, therefore, if you discover that one block is moving off on the diagonal. You will be able to straighten it.

You don't really have to worry about gauge in this project. If your particular knitting is making the block wider or narrower than the suggested 11", just change the length of each block accordingly so that each block is a square.

You can choose one or two stitch patterns that you particularly like and do the entire afghan in those stitches, switching colors every 11" (28cm). You can also make the afghan in a multitude of colors, using up scraps of yarn that you have available. Each square can be a different color and a different stitch.

Done individually, the blocks will make great throw pillows to match your afghan. Just knit two blocks according to the instructions. Join the two blocks, leaving the top open. Stuff with polyester fiberfill or foam rubber cut to size. Close the opening.

Since this afghan is going to teach you how to do a number of different stitches, a picture of how each stitch will look when it is completed appears above the instructions for that particular block.

SIZE: Approximately 44" x 66" (112cm x 167.5cm).

MATERIALS: 24 ounces aqua four-ply knitting worsted, 24 ounces royal blue four-ply knitting worsted, size 7 knitting needles, cable holder or double-pointed knitting needle, size G crochet hook (optional).

FIRST STRIP

Moss Stitch

Block One: Moss Stitch

DIRECTIONS: With royal blue, cast on 58 stitches.
Row 1: *Knit 1, purl 1.* Repeat from * to * across the row.
Row 2: *Purl 1, knit 1.* Repeat from * to * across the row.
Repeat these 2 rows until the square measures 11" (28cm).

Garter Stitch

Block Two: Garter Stitch

DIRECTIONS: Cut royal blue and attach aqua.
Row 1: Knit.
Row 2: Knit.
Repeat these 2 rows until the square measures 11" (28cm).

Stockinette Stitch

Block Three: Stockinette Stitch

DIRECTIONS: Cut aqua and attach royal blue.
Row 1: Knit.
Row 2: Purl.
Repeat these 2 rows until the square measures 11" (28cm).

Reverse Stockinette Stitch

Block Four: Reverse Stockinette Stitch

DIRECTIONS: Cut royal blue and attach aqua.
Row 1: Purl.
Row 2: Knit.
Repeat these 2 rows until the square measures 11″ (28cm).
This stitch is just what the name implies: the reverse of the stich used in Block Three.

Ridged Rib Stitch

Block Five: Ridged Rib Stitch

DIRECTIONS: Cut aqua and attach royal blue.

Row 1: Knit.	**Row 7:** Purl.
Row 2: Purl.	**Row 8:** Knit.
Row 3: Knit.	**Row 9:** Purl.
Row 4: Purl.	**Row 10:** Knit.
Row 5: Knit.	**Row 11:** Purl.
Row 6: Purl.	**Row 12:** Knit.

Repeat these 12 rows until the square measures 11″ (28cm). In the sample afghan, these 12 rows were repeated 5 times and the block completed with rows 1–6.

Basket-Weave Stitch

Block Six: Basket-Weave Stitch

DIRECTIONS: Cut royal blue and attach aqua.
Row 1: Knit 8, (purl 6, knit 6) 3 times, purl 6, knit 8.
Row 2: Purl 8, (knit 6, purl 6) 3 times, knit 6, purl 8.
Rows 3, 5, and 7: Repeat row 1.
Rows 4 and 6: Repeat row 2.
Repeat these 7 rows until the square measures 11″ (28cm). In the sample afghan, these 7 rows were repeated 10 times.
Bind off the strip.

SECOND STRIP

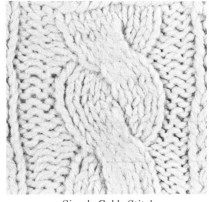
Simple Cable Stitch

Block One: Simple Cable Stitch

DIRECTIONS: With aqua, cast on 58 stitches.
Rows 1, 3 and 5: Knit 4, purl 3, knit 8, purl 3, knit 22, purl 3, knit 8, purl 3, knit 4.
Rows 2, 4 and 6: Purl 4, knit 3, purl 8, knit 3, purl 22, knit 3, purl 8, knit 3, purl 4.
Row 7: Knit 4, purl 3, slip the next 4 stitches onto a cable holder or double-pointed needle and leave at the front of the work, knit 4, knit the 4 stitches from the cable holder or double-pointed needle, purl 3, knit 22, purl 3, slip the next 4 stitches onto a cable holder or double-pointed needle and leave at the front of the work, knit 4, knit the 4 stitches from the cable holder or double-pointed needle, purl 3, knit 4.
Row 8: Repeat row 2.
Repeat these 8 rows until the square measures 11″ (28cm).

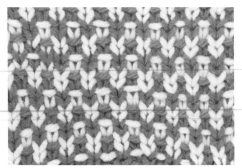
Woven Stitch

Block Two: Woven Stitch

DIRECTIONS: Attach royal blue and work this block and the next three blocks with two colors. Note that the color not in use is not carried across the row but is left at the side.

Row 1 (royal blue): *Knit 1, wool forward, slip 1 as if to purl, wool back.* Repeat from * to * across the row.

Row 2 (royal blue): Purl.

Row 3 (aqua): *Knit 1, wool forward, slip 1 as if to purl, wool back.* Repeat from * to * across the row.

Row 4 (aqua): Purl.

Repeat these 4 rows until the square measures 11″ (28cm).

Honeycomb Stitch

Block Three: Honeycomb Stitch with Knitted Border

DIRECTIONS: Work with two colors. The color not being used is left at the side. Do not carry it across the row.

Row 1 (royal blue): Knit.

Row 2 (royal blue): Knit.

Row 3 (aqua): Knit 4. *Slip 2 as if to purl, knit 6.* Repeat from * to * to the last 6 stitches. Slip 2 as if to purl, knit 4.

Row 4 (aqua): Knit 2, purl 2. *Slip 2 as if to purl (the same 2 stitches as were slipped in the previous row), purl 6.* Repeat from * to * to the last 6 stitches. Slip 2 as if to purl, purl 2, knit 2.

Rows 5 and 7 (aqua): Knit 4. *Slip 2 as if to purl, knit 6.* Repeat from * to * to the last 6 stitches. Slip 2 as if to purl, knit 4.

Rows 6 and 8 (aqua): Knit 2, purl 2. *Slip 2 as if to purl (the same 2 stitches as were slipped in the previous row), purl 6.* Repeat from * to * to the last 6 stitches. Slip 2 as if to purl, purl 2, knit 2.

Row 9 (royal blue): Knit all of the stitches, including the slipped stitches.

Rows 10, 11 and 12 (royal blue): Knit.

Rows 13, 15 and 17 (aqua): Knit 8. *Slip 2 as if to purl, knit 6.* Repeat from * to * to the last 2 stitches. Knit 2.

Rows 14, 16 and 18 (aqua): Knit 2, purl 6. *Slip 2 as if to purl, purl 6.* Repeat from * to * to the last 2 stitches. Knit 2.

Row 19 (royal blue): Knit all of the stitches, including the slipped stitches.

Rows 20, 21 and 22 (royal blue): Knit.

Repeat from row 3 until the square measures 11″ (28cm). If you wish to use the honeycomb stitch without the knitted border for another project, eliminate the 2 knit stitches from the beginning and end of each row. If you wish the end of the pattern to correspond with the beginning, bind off on row 12.

Mock Houndstooth Stitch

Block Four: Mock Houndstooth Stitch

DIRECTIONS: Work with two colors. The color not in use is left at the side. Do not carry it across the row.

Row 1 (aqua): Knit 1. *Slip 1 as if to purl, knit 2.* Repeat from * to * across the row.

Row 2 (aqua): Purl.

Row 3 (royal blue): Knit 1. *Knit 2, slip 1 as if to purl.* Repeat from * to * across the row.

Row 4 (royal blue): Purl.

Repeat these 4 rows until the square measures 11″ (28cm).

Two-Color Ladder Stitch

Block Five: Two-Color Ladder Stitch

DIRECTIONS: Work with two colors. The color not in use is left at the side. Do not carry it across the row.

Row 1 (aqua): Knit 2. *Slip 1 as if to purl, knit 5.* Repeat from * to * to the last 2 stitches. Slip 1 as if to purl, knit into the front and the back of the next stitch to increase the number of stitches to 59.

Row 2 (aqua): Purl, slipping the slipped stitches of the previous row.

Row 3 (royal blue): *Knit 5, slip 1 as if to purl.* Repeat from * to * to the last 5 stitches. Knit 5.

Row 4 (royal blue): *Knit 5, wool forward, slip 1 as if to purl, wool back.* Repeat from * to * to the last 5 stitches. Knit 5.

Row 5 (aqua): Knit 2. *Slip 1 as if to purl, knit 5.* Repeat from * to * to the last 3 stitches. Slip 1 as if to purl, knit 2.

Repeat rows 2, 3, 4 and 5 until the square measures 11″ (28cm).

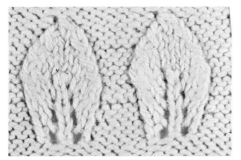

Raised Leaf Stitch

Block Six: Raised Leaf Stitch with Knitted Border

DIRECTIONS: Cut the aqua and work this block with royal blue only.

Row 1: Knit 2, purl 6. *Yarn over, knit 1, yarn over, purl 6.* Repeat from * to * to the last 2 stitches. Knit 2.

Row 2: Knit 2. *Knit 6, purl 3.* Repeat from * to * to the last 8 stitches. Knit 8.

Row 3: Knit 2, purl 6. *Knit 1, yarn over, knit 1, yarn over, knit 1, purl 6.* Repeat from * to * to the last 2 stitches. Knit 2.

Row 4: Knit 2. *Knit 6, purl 5.* Repeat from * to * to the last 8 stitches. Knit 8.

Row 5: Knit 2, purl 6. *Knit 2, yarn over, knit 1, yarn over, knit 2, purl 6.* Repeat from * to * to the last 2 stitches. Knit 2.

Row 6: Knit 2. *Knit 6, purl 7.* Repeat from * to * to the last 8 stitches. Knit 8.

Row 7: Knit 2, purl 6. *Knit 3, yarn over, knit 1, yarn over, knit 3, purl 6.* Repeat from * to * to the last 2 stitches. Knit 2.

Row 8: Knit 2. *Knit 6, purl 9.* Repeat from * to * to the last 8 stitches. Knit 8.

Row 9: Knit 2, purl 6. *Slip 1, knit 1, pass the slip stitch over the knit stitch, knit 5, knit 2 together, purl 6.* Repeat from * to * to the last 2 stitches. Knit 2.

Row 10: Knit 2. *Knit 6, purl 7.* Repeat from * to * to the last 8 stitches. Knit 8.

Row 11: Knit 2, purl 6. *Slip 1, knit 1, pass the slip stitch over the knit stitch, knit 3, knit 2 together, purl 6.* Repeat from * to * to the last 2 stitches. Knit 2.

Row 12: Knit 2. *Knit 6, purl 5.* Repeat from * to * to the last 8 stitches. Knit 8.

Row 13: Knit 2, purl 6. *Slip 1, knit 1, pass the slip stitch over the knit stitch, knit 1, knit 2 together, purl 6.* Repeat from * to * to the last 2 stitches. Knit 2.

Row 14: Knit 2. *Knit 6, purl 3.* Repeat from * to * to the last 8 stitches. Knit 8.

Row 15: Knit 2, purl 6. *Slip 1, knit 2 together, pass the slip stitch over the knit stitch, purl 6.* Repeat from * to * to the last 2 stitches. Knit 2.

Rows 16, 18 and 20: Knit.
Rows 17 and 19: Purl.

Repeat these 20 rows until the square measures 11″ (28cm). You will probably be able to get 3 rows of leaves completed. If the square is too short, repeat rows 19 and 20 until the square is the desired length. If you wish to use the raised leaf pattern without the knitted border for another project, eliminate the 2 knit stitches from the beginning and end of each row.

Bind off the strip.

THIRD STRIP

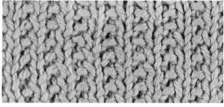

Ringwood Stitch

Block One: Ringwood Stitch

DIRECTIONS: With royal blue, cast on 58 stitches.
Row 1: Knit.
Row 2: *Knit 1, purl 1.* Repeat from * to * across the row.

Repeat these 2 rows until the square measures 11″ (28cm).

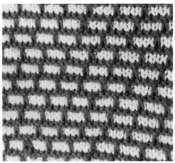

Brick Stitch

Block Two: Brick Stitch with Knitted Border

DIRECTIONS: Attach aqua and work this block and the next three blocks with two colors. Note that the color not in use is not carried across the row but is left at the side.

Row 1 (royal blue): Knit.
Row 2 (royal blue): Knit.
Row 3 (aqua): Knit 1. *Knit 3, slip 1 as if to purl.* Repeat from * to * to the last stitch. Knit 1.
Row 4 (aqua): Knit 1. *Purl, slipping the royal blue stitches of the previous row.* Repeat from * to * to the last stitch. Knit 1.
Row 5 (royal blue): Knit.
Row 6 (royal blue): Knit.
Row 7 (aqua): Knit 3. *Slip 1 as if to purl, knit 3.*

Repeat from * to * to the last 3 stitches. Slip 1, knit 2.

Row 8 (aqua): Knit 1. *Purl, slipping the royal blue stitches of the previous row.* Repeat from * to * to the last stitch. Knit 1.

Row 9 (royal blue): Knit.

Row 10 (royal blue): Knit.

Row 11 (aqua): Knit 2. *Slip 1 as if to purl, knit 3.* Repeat from * to * to the last 4 stitches. Slip 1, knit 3.

Row 12 (aqua): Knit 1. *Purl, slipping the royal blue stitches of the previous row.* Repeat from * to * to the last stitch. Knit 1.

Row 13 (royal blue): Knit.

Row 14 (royal blue): Knit.

Row 15 (aqua): Knit 1. *Slip 1 as if to purl, knit 3.* Repeat from * to * to the last stitch. Knit 1.

Row 16 (aqua): Knit 1. *Purl, slipping the royal blue stitches of the previous row.* Repeat from * to * to the last stitch. Knit 1.

Repeat these 16 rows until the square measures 11″ (28cm). If you wish to use the brick stitch without the knitted border for another project, eliminate 1 knit stitch from the beginning and end of each row.

Sand Stitch

Block Three: Sand Stitch

DIRECTIONS: Work with two colors. The color not being used is left at the side. Do not carry it across the row.

Row 1 (aqua): Knit.

Row 2 (aqua): Purl.

Row 3 (royal blue): Knit 1. *Slip 1 as if to purl, knit 1.* Repeat from * to * to the last stitch. Knit 1.

Row 4 (royal blue): Knit 1. *Knit 1, wool forward, slip 1 as if to purl, wool back.* Repeat from * to * to the last stitch. Knit 1.

Repeat these 4 rows until the square measures 11″ (28cm).

Mock Tweed Stitch

Block Four: Mock Tweed Stitch

DIRECTIONS: Work with two colors. The color not being used is left at the side. Do not carry it across the row.

Row 1 (aqua): *Slip 1 as if to purl, knit 2.* Repeat from * to * to the last 4 stitches. Slip 1, knit 1, knit 2 together. (57 stitches)

Row 2 (aqua): Knit.

Row 3 (royal blue): *Knit 2, slip 1 as if to purl.* Repeat from * to * across the row.

Row 4 (royal blue): Knit.

Row 5 (aqua): *Slip 1 as if to purl, knit 2.* Repeat from * to * across the row.

Repeat rows 2, 3, 4 and 5 until the square measures 11″ (28cm).

Half-Linen Stitch

Block Five: Half-Linen Stitch

DIRECTIONS: Work with two colors. The color not being used is left at the side. Do not carry it across the row.

Row 1 (royal blue): *Knit 1, wool forward, slip 1 as if to purl, wool back.* Repeat from * to * to the last stitch. Work twice in the last stitch by knitting into the front and the back of the stitch, wool forward, slip the loop off the left-hand needle, wool back. (58 stitches)

Row 2 (royal blue): Purl.

Row 3 (aqua): Knit 1. *Knit 1, wool forward, slip 1 as if to purl, wool back.* Repeat from * to * to the last stitch. Knit 1.

Row 4 (aqua): Purl.

Row 5 (royal blue): *Knit 1, wool forward, slip 1 as if to purl, wool back.* Repeat from * to * across the row.

Repeat rows 2, 3, 4 and 5 until the square measures 11″ (28cm).

Fancy Stitch

Block Six: Fancy Stitch

DIRECTIONS: Cut royal blue and work this block with aqua only.
Row 1: Knit, ending with a knit 2 together. (57 stitches)
Row 2: Purl.
Row 3: *Knit 1, yarn over, knit 2 together.* Repeat from * to * across the row.
Row 4: Purl.
Repeat rows 3 and 4 until the square measures 11″ (28cm). This stitch will cause the square to slant, and extra care will be necessary when blocking the square. Bind off the strip.

FOURTH STRIP

Star Stitch

Block One: Star Stitch

DIRECTIONS: With aqua, cast on 58 stitches.
Row 1: Purl. (*Note: This is the wrong side of the work.*)
Row 2: Knit 1. *Yarn over, knit 3, pass the first of the 3 knit stitches over the second and third stitches.* Repeat from * to * across the row.
Row 3: Purl.
Row 4: *Yarn over, knit 3, pass the first of the 3 knit stitches over the second and third stitches.* Repeat from * to * to the last stitch. Knit 1.
Row 5: Purl.
Row 6: Knit 2. *Yarn over, knit 3, pass the first of the 3 knit stitches over the second and third stitches.* Repeat from * to * to the last 2 stitches. Yarn over, knit 2 together.
Repeat rows 1, 2, 3, 4, 5, and 6 until the square measures 11″ (28cm). Before beginning the next square, purl 1 row. This stitch will cause the square to slant, and extra care will be necessary when blocking the square.

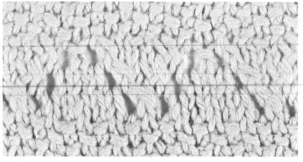

Lace and Seed Stitch

Block Two: Lace and Seed Stitch

DIRECTIONS: Cut aqua and attach royal blue.
Row 1: Knit 1. *Purl 1, knit 1.* Repeat from * to * to the last 2 stitches. Knit 2 together. (57 stitches)
Row 2: Knit 1. *Purl 1, knit 1.* Repeat from * to * across the row.
Rows 3, 4, 5 and 6: Repeat row 2.
Row 7: Knit 1. *Yarn over, slip 1 as if to purl, knit 1, pass the slip stitch over the knit stitch, knit 3, knit 2 together, yarn over, knit 1.* Repeat from * to * across the row.
Rows 8, 10, and 12: Purl.
Row 9: Knit 2. *Yarn over, slip 1 as if to purl, knit 1, pass the slip stitch over the knit stitch, knit 1, knit 2 together, yarn over, knit 3.* Repeat from * to * across the row, ending with a knit 2 instead of a knit 3.
Row 11: Knit 3. *Yarn over, slip 1 as if to purl, knit 2 together, pass the slip stitch over the knit stitch, yarn over, knit 5.* Repeat from * to * across the row, ending with a knit 3 instead of a knit 5.
Repeat these 12 rows until the square measures 11″ (28cm). On the repeats, do not decrease again in row 1, but use the row 2 instructions for the first 6 rows. In the sample afghan, the 12 rows were repeated 6 times.

Broken Rib Stitch

Block Three: Broken Rib Stitch

DIRECTIONS: Cut royal blue and attach aqua.
Row 1: Purl 1, purl into the front and the back of the stitch. *(Knit into the front and the back of the stitch) 2 times, purl 2.* Repeat from * to * across the row. (*Note: The increase in the second purl stitch is used only once; use the instructions for row 3 for this row on the repeats.*) (58 stitches)
Rows 2, 4 and 6: Knit 2. *(Purl 2 together) 2 times, knit 2.* Repeat from * to * across the row.
Rows 3 and 5: Purl 2. *(Knit into the back and the front of the stitch) 2 times, purl 2.* Repeat from * to * across the row.
Rows 7, 9 and 11: (Knit into the back and the front of the stitch) 2 times. *Purl 2 (knit into the back and the front of the stitch) 2 times.* Repeat from * to * across the row.
Rows 8, 10 and 12: (Purl 2 together) 2 times. *Knit 2, (purl 2 together) 2 times.* Repeat from * to * across the row.
Repeat these 12 rows until the square measures 11″ (28cm). On the repeats do not increase again in row 1, but use the instructions for row 3 for the first row.

Butterfly Stitch

Block Four: Butterfly Stitch

DIRECTIONS: Cut aqua and attach royal blue.
Row 1: Knit across the row, knitting into the back and the front of the first and last stitch. (60 stitches)
Row 2: Purl.
Rows 3 and 5: *Knit 2 together, yarn over, knit 1, yarn over, slip 1 as if to purl, knit 1, pass the slip stitch over the knit stitch, knit 5.* Repeat from * to * across the row.
Rows 4 and 6: *Purl 7, slip 1 as if to purl, purl 2.* Repeat from * to * across the row.
Row 7: Knit.
Row 8: Purl.
Row 9: *Knit 5, knit 2 together, yarn over, knit 1, yarn over, slip 1, knit 1, pass the slip stitch over the knit stitch.* Repeat from * to * across the row.
Row 10: *Purl 2, slip 1 as if to purl, purl 7.* Repeat from * to * across the row.
Row 11: *Knit 5, knit 2 together, yarn over, knit 1, yarn over, slip 1 as if to purl, knit 1, pass the slip stitch over the knit stitch.* Repeat from * to * across the row.
Row 12: *Purl 2, slip 1 as if to purl, purl 7.* Repeat from * to * across the row.
Row 13: Knit.
Row 14: Purl.
Repeat from row 3 until the square measures 11″ (28cm).

Openwork Slip Stitch

Block Five: Openwork Slip Stitch

DIRECTIONS: Cut royal blue and attach aqua.
Row 1: Knit.
Row 2: *Purl 4, yarn over.* Repeat from * to * across the row.
Row 3: *Allow the yarn over of the previous row to slip off the needle, yarn over, slip 1 as if to purl, knit 3, pass the slip stitch over the 3 knitted stitches.* Repeat from * to * across the row.
Row 4: Purl.
Repeat these 4 rows until the square measures 11″ (28cm).

Ridged Slip Stitch

Block Six: Ridged Slip Stitch

DIRECTIONS: Cut aqua and attach royal blue.
Row 1: *Knit 3, slip 1 as if to purl.* Repeat from * to * across the row.
Row 2: *Slip 1 as if to purl, purl 3.* Repeat from * to * across the row.
Row 3: *Knit 3, slip 1 as if to purl.* Repeat from * to * across the row.
Row 4: Knit.
Row 5: *Knit 1, slip 1 as if to purl, knit 2.* Repeat from * to * across the row.
Row 6: *Purl 2, slip 1 as if to purl, purl 1.* Repeat from * to * across the row.
Row 7: *Knit 1, slip 1 as if to purl, knit 2.* Repeat from * to * across the row.
Row 8: Knit.
Repeat these 8 rows until the square measures 11″ (28cm).
Bind off strip.

FINISHING: Finish following the suggestions in the "Hints on Finishing" section in the appendix. Block the strips, making certain that each square is 11″ (28cm). Join the strips. If desired, make a border of single crochet around the edges of the afghan.

WARM-ALL

What probably first inspired me to make this "Warm-all" was the memory of those white sheets on my mother's furniture. If you like to keep your furniture covered, why not throw a Warm-all over a chair or a couch. The lacy knitted fabric will protect the furniture but will still allow the lovely color and texture of your upholstery to peek through. If you use one of the current man-made threads to knit the Warm-all, it will be washable and can be easily laundered when dirty, thereby preserving the upholstery.

A Warm-all, as the name implies, envelopes you with warmth when you sit wrapped in it. Curl up on the couch in your cool living room and throw the Warm-all all about you. Despite its fragile look, the Warm-all is extravagantly warm.

I like to adapt knitting patterns so they can be used for all kinds of projects. If you make the Warm-all a little shorter, it becomes an excellent stole to wear over your summer dresses on those evenings when air-conditioning turns a warm night into an arctic freeze. You can change the width of a Warm-all by casting on fewer multiples of 17 stitches (which is the lace pattern). Made a little larger, the Warm-all can become a bedspread.

SIZE: Approximately 36″ x 88″ (91.5cm x 223.5cm).

MATERIALS: 24 ounces four-ply knitting worsted, size 15 knitting needles, tapestry needle.

DIRECTIONS: Cast on 112 stitches.
Rows 1, 2, 3, 4, 5, and 6: Knit.
Row 7: Knit 5. *(Purl 2 together) 3 times, (yarn over, knit 1) 5 times, yarn over, (purl 2 together) 3 times.* Repeat from * to * to the last 5 stitches. Knit 5.
Row 8: Knit 5, purl 102, knit 5.
Row 9: Knit.
Row 10: Knit 5, purl 102, knit 5.
Repeat rows 7, 8, 9 and 10 until the piece is the desired length, ending with row 7 of the pattern. Knit 6 rows and bind off loosely.

FINISHING: Finish following the suggestions in the "Hints on Finishing" section in the appendix. If desired, make seven 9″ (23cm) tassles according to the directions given in the appendix and attach with a tapestry needle to each point at the bottom and top.

THE LUNCHEON SET   (*see page 18*)

OVAL PLACE MAT   (*see page 22*)

THE WORLD'S EASIEST LACE TABLECLOTH (*see page 24*)

POT HOLDERS AND RACK (*see page 30*)

VEGETABLE BAGS (*see page 32*)

RIPPLE AFGHAN   (*see page 36*)   LACE CURTAINS   (*see page 53*)

AFRICAN VIOLET POT COVER   (*see page 52*)

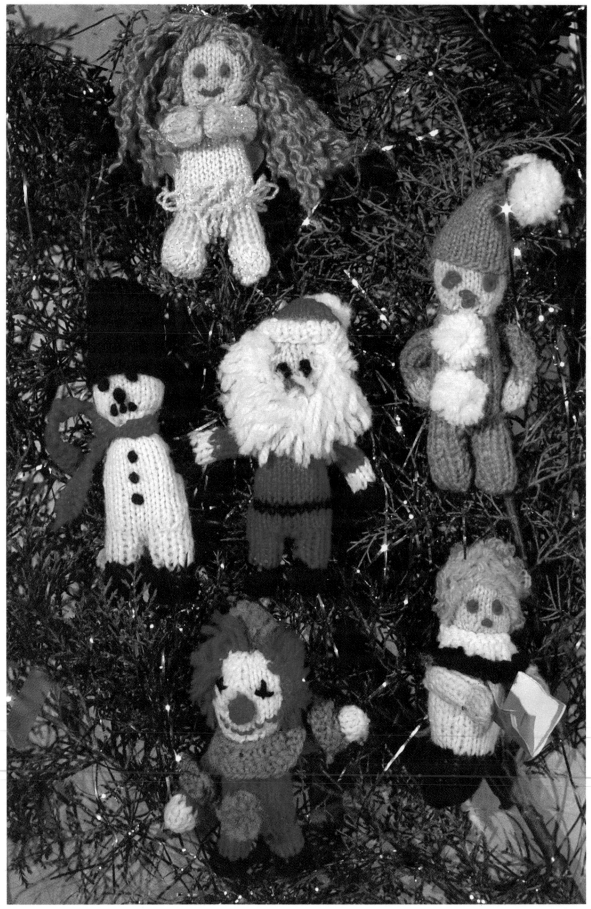

CHRISTMAS ORNAMENTS (*see page 71*)

THE NOSTALGIA DOILY

I have never been able to explain the continuing popularity of the simple doily. Even I, who love modern furniture and the latest music, can find something romantic and appealing in a doily. Perhaps it is because a doily represents another age, a time when things were simpler and we had time for lovely bits of lace. Surely the doily reminds me of the living room of my childhood, where each lamp and each vase sat on its own doily rather than directly on the table. In my child's mind I thought that putting a lamp down on a table without a doily underneath was almost as big a crime as taking the tags off pillows—those tags that stated "Do not remove under penalty of. . . ."

Most of the old doilies you now see in antique shops are crocheted doilies. For some reason, we knitters allow the crocheters to keep the delight of making handmade lace as their own special pleasure. You *can* make beautiful doilies with your knitting needles. You will have to follow the instructions very carefully, however, making certain that you don't lose your place or any of your stitches along the way.

If you have never knitted a doily in the round before, read the special instructions given in the appendix. Note that the entire doily—including the border—is knitted!

SIZE: Approximately 9 1/2'' in diameter (24cm).

MATERIALS: One 218-yard (200m) ball DMC Brilliant Crochet Cotton, size 4 double-pointed knitting needles (set of four), size 4 circular knitting needle.

NOTE: Always mark the start of each round by placing a safety pin in the first stitch of the round. Move the pin when you reach this stitch and replace it in the new stitch just formed.

DIRECTIONS: Cast 9 stitches onto one double-pointed needle. Divide the stitches onto three needles; join, being careful not to twist the stitches.

Rounds 1 and 2: Knit.

Round 3: *Yarn over, knit 1.* Repeat from * to * around the round. (18 stitches)

Rounds 4, 5 and 6: Knit.

Round 7: *Yarn over, knit 1.* Repeat from * to * around the round. (36 stitches)

Rounds 8, 9 and 10: Knit.

Round 11: Knit 1. *Yarn over, knit 1, yarn over, knit 3.* Repeat from * to * to the last 3 stitches. Yarn over, knit 1, yarn over, knit 2. (54 stitches)

Rounds 12, 13 and 14: Knit.

Round 15: Purl 1. *(Yarn over, knit 1) 3 times, yarn over, purl 3.* Repeat from * to * to the last 2 stitches. Yarn over, purl 2. (90 stitches)

Rounds 16, 17 and 18: Knit.

Round 19: *Purl 1, purl 2 together, (yarn over, knit 1) 3 times, yarn over, (purl 2 together) 2 times.* Repeat from * to * around the round to the last 2 stitches. Yarn over, purl 2. (99 stitches)

Rounds 20, 21 and 22: Knit.

Round 23: *(Purl 2 together) 2 times, (yarn over, knit 1) 3 times, yarn over, (purl 2 together) 2 times.* Repeat from * to * around the round. (99 stitches)

Rounds 24, 25 and 26: Knit.

Rounds 27 and 31: Repeat round 23.

Rounds 28, 29, 30, 32, 33 and 34: Knit.

Round 35: *Purl 2 together, purl 1, (yarn over, knit 1) 5 times, yarn over, purl 1, purl 2 together.* Repeat from * to * around the round. (135 stitches)

Rounds 36, 37 and 38: Knit.

Round 39: *Purl 2, (yarn over, knit 1) 11 times, yarn over, purl 2.* Repeat from * to * around the round. (243 stitches)

Rounds 40, 41 and 42: Knit.

Round 43: Knit 1. *Knit 2 together, yarn over, knit 2 together; turn, purl 1, work 5 stitches in the next stitch— *to work 5 stitches in 1 stitch (knit 1, purl 1) 2 times, knit 1 in the same stitch—* purl 1, slip 1 as if to purl; turn, bind off 7 stitches (1 stitch will remain on the right-hand needle).* Repeat from * to * around the round until there are 2 stitches remaining on the left-hand needle. Then knit 1, yarn over, knit 1; turn, purl 1, work 5 stitches in the next stitch, purl 1, slip 1; turn, bind off the remaining stitches and fasten off.

FINISHING: Finish following the special suggestions for finishing lace projects in the "Hints on Finishing" section in the appendix. Be sure to pin at frequent intervals around the entire knitted border.

OLD-FASHIONED DOILY BROUGHT UP-TO-DATE

Most old-fashioned doilies were made with white or ecru thread. But if you're like I am and like both modern furniture and old-fashioned doilies, why not make your doily in a bright, modern color to match the daring colors in a modern room. A vivid spot of orange on a stark white table provides a decorating conversation piece, particularly when your guests realize that the spot of color is "one of those doilies my aunt used to have all over her house."

This doily is actually my adaptation of a doily I found in an antique shop. If you have never knitted a doily in the round, read the special instructions given in the appendix.

SIZE: Approximately 13 1/2″ in diameter (33cm).

MATERIALS: One 218-yard (200m) ball DMC Brilliant Crochet Cotton, size 4 double-pointed knitting needles (set of four), size 4 circular needle.

NOTE: Always mark the start of each round by placing a safety pin in the first stitch of the round. Move the pin when you reach this stitch and replace it in the new stitch just formed.

DIRECTIONS: Cast 6 stitches onto one double-pointed needle. Divide the stitches evenly onto three needles; join, being careful not to twist the stitches.

Round 1: Knit.

Round 2: *Knit 1, yarn over.* Repeat from * to * around the round. (12 stitches)

Round 3: *Knit in the front and the back of the stitch, yarn over, knit and purl into the stitch, yarn over.* Repeat from * to * around the round. (36 stitches)

Round 4: Knit.

Round 5: *Knit in the back of the stitch, yarn over, knit 5, yarn over.* Repeat from * to * around the round. (48 stitches)

Round 6: Knit.

Round 7: *Knit in the back of the stitch, yarn over, knit 7, yarn over.* Repeat from * to * around the round. (60 stitches)

Round 8: Knit.

Round 9: *Knit in the back of the stitch, yarn over, knit 9, yarn over.* Repeat from * to * around the round. (72 stitches)

Round 10: Knit.

Round 11: *Knit in the back of the stitch, yarn over, knit 11, yarn over.* Repeat from * to * around the round. (84 stitches)

Round 12: Knit.

Round 13: *Knit in the back of the stitch, (yarn over, knit 2 together) 3 times, yarn over, knit 1, (yarn over, slip 1, knit 1, pass the slip stitch over the knit stitch) 3 times, yarn over.* Repeat from * to * around the round. (96 stitches)

Round 14: Knit.

Round 15: *Knit in the back of the stitch, (yarn over, knit 2 together) 3 times, yarn over, knit 3, (yarn over, slip 1 as if to purl, knit 1, pass the slip stitch over the knit stitch) 3 times, yarn over.* Repeat from * to * around the round. (108 stitches)

Round 16: Knit.

Round 17: *Knit in the back of the stitch, (yarn over, knit 2 together) 4 times, yarn over, knit 1, (yarn over, slip 1 as if to purl, knit 1, pass the slip stitch over the knit stitch) 4 times, yarn over.* Repeat from * to * around the round. (120 stitches)

Round 18: Knit.

Round 19: *Yarn over, knit in the back of the stitch, (yarn over, knit 2 together) 4 times, yarn over, knit 3 together, (yarn over, slip 1 as if to purl, knit 1, pass the slip stitch over the knit stitch) 4 times.* Repeat from * to * around the round. (120 stitches)

Round 20: Knit.

Round 21: *Yarn over, knit 3, yarn over, slip 1 as if to purl, knit 1, pass the slip stitch over the knit stitch, yarn over, knit 3 together, yarn over, knit 2 together, yarn over, knit 3, yarn over, slip 1 as if to purl, knit 1, pass the slip stitch over the knit stitch, yarn over, knit 3 together, yarn over, knit 2 together.* Repeat from * to * around the round. (120 stitches)

Round 22: Knit.

Round 23: *Yarn over, knit 5, yarn over, slip 1 as if to purl, knit 1, pass the slip stitch over the knit stitch, knit 1, knit 2 together.* Repeat from * to * around the round. (120 stitches)

Round 24: Knit.

Round 25: *Yarn over, knit 7, yarn over, knit 3 together.* Repeat from * to * around the round. (120 stitches)

Round 26: Knit.

Round 27: *Knit 5, (yarn over) 4 times, knit 5.* Repeat from * to * around the round. (168 stitches)

Round 28: *Knit 5, work 9 stitches in the first yarn over—to work 9 stitches in 1 stitch (knit 1, purl 1) 4 times, knit 1 in the same stitch—allow the 3 other yarn overs to slip off the left-hand needle, knit 5.* Repeat from * to * around the round. (228 stitches)

Round 29: *Knit 5, yarn over, knit 9, yarn over, knit 5.* Repeat from * to * around the round. (252 stitches)

Round 30: Knit.

Round 31: *Knit 5, yarn over, knit 11, yarn over, knit 5.* Repeat from * to * around the round. (276 stitches)

Round 32: Knit.

Round 33: *Knit 3, (knit 2 together, yarn over) 4 times, knit 1, (yarn over, slip 1 as if to purl, knit 1, pass the slip stitch over the knit stitch) 4 times, knit 3.* Repeat from * to * around the round. (276 stitches)

Round 34: Knit.

Round 35: *Knit 2, (knit 2 together, yarn over) 4 times, knit 3 (yarn over, slip 1 as if to purl, knit 1, pass the slip stitch over the knit stitch) 4 times, knit 2.* Repeat from * to * around the round. (276 stitches)

Round 36: Knit.

Round 37: *Knit 1, (knit 2 together, yarn over) 5 times, work 3 stitches in the next stitch—to work 3 stitches in 1 stitch, knit 1, purl 1, knit 1 in the same stitch—(yarn over, slip 1 as if to purl, knit 1, pass the slip stitch over the knit stitch) 5 times, knit 1.* Repeat from * to * around the round. (300 stitches)

Round 38: Knit.

Round 39: *(Knit 2 together, yarn over) 5 times, knit 5, (yarn over, slip 1 as if to purl, knit 1, pass the slip stitch over the knit stitch) 5 times.* Repeat from * to * around the round. (300 stitches)

Round 40: Knit.

Bind off loosely.

FINISHING: Finish following the special suggestions for finishing lace projects in the "Hints on Finishing" section in the appendix. This doily will require careful blocking to shape all of the points of the star properly. Wash the doily and pin it into shape on a flat surface, gently pulling the twelve little points until the star shape is in position.

their renditions of "Für Elise," the Spanish shawl and family portraits were whisked off the piano, to be carefully replaced only after the third encore of "The Happy Farmer."

I remember hours of sitting in my Sunday-best staring at the flung-aside Spanish shawl and thinking of how I'd much prefer to wrap myself in it and dance a tarantella rather than to sit listening to the plink plank of an out-of-tune piano. Even after the shawl had been returned to its place on the piano, I'd dream of trips to sunny Spain, wrapped in my Spanish shawl, conquering the hearts of dark, millionaire Spanish noblemen. A Spanish shawl always seemed to me to be too romantic an objet d'art to spend its lifetime covering a rarely used piano.

I don't have a grand piano in my living room, but one of my friends, who is a professional musician, has one, and it brings be much pleasure to see a Spanish shawl on her piano. It belongs on a living room piano, if only to give a new generation of little girls something to pin a dream upon. In case you don't have a place for a Spanish shawl in your living room, why not make this shawl and wear it the next time you spend an evening with that dark, millionaire Spanish nobleman or his substitute.

This shawl is actually very simple to make. The lace section is just a variation of the old knit stitch. You insert the needle into the stitch as if you were knitting, but don't take the stitch off the needle. Instead, wrap the thread around the needle 3 times and then complete the stitch. On the return row, knit 1 stitch, allowing the extra wraps to fall off the needle.

I find it easier to work this project on a circular needle rather than on straight needles (knitting back and forth in rows, of course, rather than in rounds) because of the large number of stitches that must be placed on the needle.

SIZE: Approximately 70″ x 50″ (178cm x 127cm).

MATERIALS: 16 ounces black four-ply knitting worsted, size 11 knitting needles.

DIRECTIONS: Cast on 4 stitches.
Row 1: Knit across the row, increasing 1 stitch at the beginning and end of the row by knitting into the front and the back of the first and last stitch.
Row 2: Repeat row 1.
Row 3: Repeat row 1.
Row 4: *Knit, winding the thread 3 times around the needle.* Repeat from * to * across the row.
Row 5: *Knit, letting the extra wraps drop.* Repeat from * to * across the row.
Repeat these 5 rows until you have repeated the pattern 30 times (or until the shawl is the desired length). (184 stitches)
Bind off loosely.

FINISHING: Finish following the suggestions in the "Hints on Finishing" section in the appendix. Make sixty-one 5 1/2″ (14cm) fringes following the instructions for making fringes given in the appendix. Attach the fringes along both edges of row 1 along the sides of the stole, and place a fringe at the bottom point.

THE SPANISH SHAWL

The homes of well-to-do neighbors and relatives I visited as a child always boasted a grand piano. It didn't matter that no one ever played that piano; the mere presence of the behemoth announced that this was a family of culture. Since lace doilies were sprinkled on the little tables in the household, nothing less than a Spanish shawl had to be casually flung across the closed sounding board of the piano. Pictures of the family in silver frames were artistically placed upon the Spanish shawl.

On the rare occasions that the piano might be played upon by visiting children who would enthrall us with

2.

THE DINING ROOM

We were big on dining rooms in my youth. Like the living room, our dining room was used no more than four or five times each year. Every house, however, had to have a large dining room. We ate our everyday meals in the kitchen at the wooden kitchen table, which was kept covered with an oilcloth tablecloth. But, on special holidays, the dining room was opened, and the family moved into grandeur and elegance to eat around a mahogany table covered with a sparkling damask tablecloth.

We were big on family gatherings. A family didn't just consist of a mother, a father and a few children, but included aunts, uncles, cousins and unmarried friends from a parent's childhood. (I remember one year vainly trying to find out the names for the father-in-law and the mother-in-law of a cousin so that, in an essay for school, I could describe the exact relationship of every guest at our Thanksgiving dinner.) A family like that needed an enormous room with a huge table, large chairs, big bowls and lots of silverware and glasses. We needed platters sized to hold the great quantities of food that came steaming from the kitchen. Even water had to be consumed from gold-trimmed stemware. Huge buffets were needed to hold all of the dishes, silverware and glasses.

After the food was eaten, the mounds of dishes were moved into the kitchen; the tablecloth and the linen napkins were folded; the leaves were taken out of the table; the extra chairs were returned to their usual spots around the house; the carpet was neatly vacuumed; and every crumb and speck were removed. And so the dining room was put to sleep again, not to be disturbed until the next family gathering. In between family festivities the only living soul who wandered among the silent chairs standing guard over the huge lace-covered table was the perennial, solitary duster, who crawled along the floor patiently moving her cloth along the ornate rungs of the chairs.

Sometime between my childhood and the purchase of my first home, the dining room disappeared from the American home. I'm sure sociologists could explain this phenomenon. I theorize that the disappearance of the dining room followed that of the family. At some point we stopped inviting third cousins to family parties, and dinner parties changed from circuses to intimate little gatherings. We no longer needed huge tables and huge buffets to hold huge platters and mounds of dishes. Decorators convinced us that dining rooms were wasted space, unused for much of the time. They were able to convince us to give up our dining rooms only because we had already decided to give up family dining. Instead, we had the combination family room-dining room (the full-time family room masquerading as a dining room when the occasion demanded) or the L-shaped living room (the full-time living room with a small corner reserved for a postage-stamp-sized table that, through a feat of modern engineering, could open up to seat twenty very uncomfortable people).

Sometime between the blasé fifties and turbulent sixties and the changing seventies, we once again longed for the return of our dining rooms. We were no longer satisfied with our family room cum dining room or our L-shaped living room with its extension table. We began to ask for the return of the formal dining room. No matter that it was to be used only a few times a year. We wanted a room for elegance! Are we now ready to invite our cousin's father- and mother-in-law to family dinners?

My present home has a formal dining room. It doesn't matter to me that it stands idle most of the time. We don't wait for huge family gatherings to eat dinner in the dining room; the arrival home from college of a daughter is cause enough for such an occasion. We use our dining room whenever we want to feel festive or to celebrate. It can be a great occasion like New Year's Eve or simply an enjoyable dinner of rarely-served roast prime ribs. What we are celebrating doesn't matter; what matters is the desire to be elegant.

This chapter contains knitted projects for that elegant room. They are not the projects for easy, informal living—you'll find those in other chapters. These are the projects for those special moments to be savored in that room in your home which uses up space and in return allows a pauper to luxuriate like a king.

THE LUNCHEON SET

I spent many long, unhappy hours carefully pouring furniture polish over the top of my mother's dining room table and then working until my arms ached making certain that the shine of the highly polished table afforded me a view of my sweaty face. But only my mother—as she checked my work—ever saw that shine! For along with her contemporaries, my mother never served any food on her dining room table unless the table was protected by heavy padding and topped with a highly starched white tablecloth. (Of course, those were the days of laundresses and inexpensive hired help who could spend an entire day doing the ironing.) Even when the table was not used for eating, it was always covered with a beautiful lace tablecloth through which small glimpses of polished mahogany could be seen. It wasn't just style that dictated keeping a table covered. Those were the days before plastic finishes and protective waxes, and a table was covered in order to protect it.

There were a few daring hostesses who did serve their guests on mats that were akin to our modern place mats. These were called luncheon sets (luncheons were more informal than dinners and one could escape with a less formal table). A luncheon set consisted of several place mats in two or three sizes to provide each guest with a large mat for the luncheon plate, a smaller mat for the coffee cup (or the bread-and-butter dish), and a tiny mat for the drinking glass. The hostess might be serving informally, but she was sure to make certain that no piece of china rested upon her naked table.

I can't imagine anyone today wasting a beautiful luncheon set on a mere lunch—unless it were to be a very elegant affair. Somehow I can't see a typical lunch in my house (soup and a peanut butter sandwich) served on something as lovely as a luncheon set. Today's hostess probably doesn't have to worry about the finish on her table; even antique tables are often refinished to make them almost impervious to spots and stains. She can, therefore, feel free to serve the most elegant dinner on a set of place mats—and why not on this beautiful luncheon set.

You begin working each of the mats in the center with four double-pointed knitting needles. The small and the medium-sized place mats will probably have to be worked entirely on the double-pointed needles. The large mat can be started on double-pointed needles and then worked onto a circular needle at about the thirteenth or fourteenth round. If you have never worked in the round before, start with the smaller mats and by the time you begin to work on the largest place mat, you'll find that you are an "old pro." I've included some special hints on knitting in the round in the appendix.

SIZE: Large place mat: approximately 14 1/2″ (36.8cm) in diameter. Medium place mat: approximately 9″ (23cm) in diameter. Small place mat: approximately 6″ (15cm) in diameter.

MATERIALS: Two 218-yard (200m) balls DMC Brilliant Crochet Cotton (for each setting); size 3 double-pointed knitting needles (set of four), size 3 circular knitting needle.

NOTE: Always mark the start of each round by placing a safety pin in the first stitch of the round. Move the pin when you reach this stitch and replace it in the new stitch just formed.

LARGE PLACE MAT

DIRECTIONS: Cast 8 stitches onto one double-pointed needle. Divide the stitches onto three needles (put 2 stitches onto the first and third needles and 2 stitches onto the second needle.) Join, being careful not to twist the stitches.

Rounds 1 and 2: Knit.
Round 3: *Yarn over, knit 1.* Repeat from * to * around the round. (16 stitches)
Rounds 4, 5 and 6: Knit.
Round 7: *Yarn over, knit 1.* Repeat from * to * around the round. (32 stitches)
Rounds 8, 9, 10, 11 and 12: Knit.
Round 13: *Knit 2 together, (yarn over) 2 times, slip 1 as if to knit, knit 1, pass the slip stitch over the knit stitch.* Repeat from * to * around the round.
Round 14: Knit 1, allow the first yarn over to slip off the left-hand needle, work 9 stitches in the second yarn over—*to work 9 stitches in 1 stitch (knit 1, purl 1) 4 times, knit 1 in the same stitch.* *Knit 2, allow the first yarn over to slip off the left-hand needle, work 9 stitches in the next yarn over.* Repeat from * to * around the round to the last stitch. Knit 1. (88 stitches)
Rounds 15, 16 and 17: Knit.
Round 18: Knit around the round, knitting and purling into the first and last stitches. (90 stitches)
Round 19: *Purl 1, purl 2 together, (yarn over, knit 1) 3 times, yarn over, (purl 2 together) 2 times.* Repeat from * to * around the round. (99 stitches)

Rounds 20, 21 and 22: Knit.
Round 23: *(Purl 2 together) 2 times, (yarn over, knit 1) 3 times, yarn over, (purl 2 together) 2 times.* Repeat from * to * around the round. (99 stitches)
Rounds 24, 25 and 26: Knit.
Round 27: *(Purl 2 together) 2 times, (yarn over, knit 1) 3 times, yarn over, (purl 2 together) 2 times.* Repeat from * to * around the round. (99 stitches)
Rounds 28, 29 and 30: Knit.
Round 31: *(Purl 2 together) 2 times, (yarn over, knit 1) 3 times, yarn over, (purl 2 together) 2 times.* Repeat from * to * around the round. (99 stitches)
Rounds 32, 33 and 34: Knit.
Round 35: *Purl 2 together, purl 1, (yarn over, knit 1) 5 times, yarn over, purl 1, purl 2 together.* Repeat from * to * around the round. (135 stitches)
Rounds 36, 37 and 38: Knit.
Round 39: *(Purl 2 together) 2 times, purl 1, (yarn over, knit 1) 4 times, yarn over, (purl 2 together) 3 times.* Repeat from * to * around the round. (135 stitches)
Rounds 40, 41 and 42: Knit.
Round 43: *(Purl 2 together) 2 times, purl 1, (yarn over, knit 1) 4 times, yarn over, (purl 2 together) 3 times.* Repeat from * to * around the round. (135 stitches)
Rounds 44, 45 and 46: Knit.
Round 47: *(Purl 2 together) 2 times, purl 1, (yarn over, knit 1) 4 times, yarn over, (purl 2 together) 3 times.* Repeat from * to * around the round. (135 stitches)
Rounds 48, 49 and 50: Knit.
Round 51: *(Purl 2 together) 2 times, purl 1, (yarn over, knit 1) 4 times, yarn over, (purl 2 together) 3 times.* Repeat from * to * around the round. (135 stitches)
Rounds 52, 53 and 54: Knit.
Round 55: *Purl 3, (yarn over, knit 1) 9 times, yarn over, (purl 1) 3 times.* Repeat from * to * around the round. (225 stitches)
Rounds 56, 57 and 58: Knit.
Round 59: *(Purl 3 together) 2 times, purl 2 together, (yarn over, knit 1) 9 times, yarn over, purl 2 together, (purl 3 together) 2 times.* Repeat from * to * around the round. (225 stitches)
Rounds 60, 61 and 62: Knit.
Round 63: Knit 1. *Knit 2 together, yarn over, knit 2 together; turn, purl 1, work 9 stitches in the next stitch—*to work 9 stitches in 1 stitch (knit 1, purl 1) 4 times, knit 1 in the same stitch*—purl 1, slip 1 as if to purl; turn, bind off 11 stitches (1 stitch remaining on the right-hand needle).* Repeat from * to * around the round. Fasten off.

MEDIUM PLACE MAT

DIRECTIONS: Cast 8 stitches onto one double-pointed needle. Divide the stitches onto three needles (put 3 stitches onto the first and third needles and 2 stitches onto the second needle). Join, being careful not to twist the stitches.

Rounds 1 and 2: Knit.
Round 3: *Yarn over, knit 1.* Repeat from * to * around the round. (16 stitches)

Rounds 4, 5 and 6: Knit.

Round 7: *Yarn over, knit 1.* Repeat from * to * around the round. (32 stitches)

Rounds 8, 9, 10, 11 and 12: Knit.

Round 13: *Knit 2 together, (yarn over) 2 times, slip 1 as if to knit, knit 1, pass the slip stitch over the knit stitch.* Repeated from * to * around the round.

Round 14: Knit 1, allow the first yarn over to slip off the left-hand needle, work 9 stitches in the second yarn over—*to work 9 stitches in 1 stitch (knit 1, purl 1) 4 times, knit 1 in the same stitch.* *Knit 2, allow the first yarn over to slip off the left-hand needle, work 9 stitches in the next yarn over.* Repeat from * to * around the round to the last stitch. Knit 1. (88 stitches)

Rounds 15, 16 and 17: Knit.

Round 18: Knit around the round, knitting and purling into the first and last stitches. (90 stitches)

Round 19: *Purl 1, purl 2 together, (yarn over, knit 1) 3 times, yarn over, (purl 2 together) 2 times.* Repeat from * to * around the round. (99 stitches)

Rounds 20, 21 and 22: Knit.

Round 23: *(Purl 2 together) 2 times, (yarn over, knit 1) 3 times, yarn over, (purl 2 together) 2 times.* Repeat from * to * around the round. (99 stitches)

Rounds 24, 25 and 26: Knit.

Round 27: *(Purl 2 together) 2 times, (yarn over, knit 1) 3 times, yarn over, (purl 2 together) 2 times.* Repeat from * to * around the round. (99 stitches)

Rounds 28, 29 and 30: Knit.

Round 31: *(Purl 2 together) 2 times, (yarn over, knit 1) 3 times, yarn over, (purl 2 together) 2 times.* Repeat from * to * around the round. (99 stitches)

Rounds 32, 33 and 34: Knit.

Round 35: *Purl 2 together, purl 1, (yarn over, knit 1) 5 times, yarn over, purl 1, purl 2 together.* Repeat from * to * around the round. (135 stitches)

Round 36: Knit.

Round 37: Knit 1. *Knit 2 together, yarn over, knit 2 together; turn, purl 1, work 9 stitches in 1 stitch—*to work 9 stitches in 1 stitch (knit 1, purl 1) 4 times, knit 1 in the same stitch*—purl 1, slip 1 as if to purl; turn, bind off 11 stitches (1 stitch remaining on the right-hand needle).* Repeat from * to * to the last 5 stitches. Knit 1, yarn over, knit 2 together; turn, purl 1, work 9 stitches in the next stitch, purl 1, slip 1 as if to purl; turn, bind off 11 stitches, knit 1, yarn over, knit 1; turn, purl 1, work 9 stitches in the next stitch, purl 1, slip 1 as if to purl; turn, bind off the remaining stitches. Fasten off.

SMALL PLACE MAT

DIRECTIONS: Cast 8 stitches onto one double-pointed needle. Divide the stitches onto three needles (put 3 stitches onto the first and third needles and 2 stitches onto the second needle). Join, being careful not to twist the stitches.

Rounds 1 and 2: Knit.

Round 3: *Yarn over, knit 1.* Repeat from * to * around the round. (16 stitches)

Rounds 4, 5 and 6: Knit.

Round 7: *Yarn over, knit 1.* Repeat from * to * around the round. (32 stitches)

Rounds 8, 9, 10, 11 and 12: Knit.

Round 13: *Knit 2 together, (yarn over) 2 times, slip 1 as if to knit, knit 1, pass the slip stitch over the knit stitch.* Repeat from * to * around the round.

Round 14: Knit 1, allow the first yarn over to slip off the left-hand needle, work 9 stitches in the second yarn over—*to work 9 stitches in 1 stitch (knit 1, purl 1) 4 times, knit 1 in the same stitch. *Knit 2, allow the first yarn over to slip off the left-hand needle, work 9 stitches in the next stitch.* Repeat from * to * around the round to the last stitch. Knit 1. (88 stitches)

Rounds 15, 16 and 17: Knit.

Round 18: Knit around the round, knitting and purling into the first and last stitches. (90 stitches)

Round 19: *Purl 1, purl 2 together, (yarn over, knit 1) 3 times, yarn over, (purl 2 together) 2 times.* Repeat from * to * around the round. (99 stitches)

Rounds 20, 21 and 22: Knit.

Round 23: Knit 1. *Knit 2 together, yarn over, knit 2 together; turn, purl 1, work 9 stitches in the next stitch—*to work 9 stitches in 1 stitch (knit 1, purl 1) 4 times, knit 1 in the same stitch*—purl 1, slip 1 as if to purl; turn, bind off 11 stitches (1 stitch remaining on the right-hand needle).* Repeat from * to * around the round to the last 3 stitches. Knit 2 together, yarn over, knit 1; turn, purl 1, work 9 stitches in the next stitch, purl 1, slip 1 as if to purl; turn, bind off the remaining stitches. Fasten off.

FINISHING: Finish each of the mats following the special suggestions for finishing lace projects in the "Hints on Finishing" section in the appendix. Be sure to pin at frequent intervals around the entire knitted border of each of the mats.

RECTANGULAR PLACE MAT

If you are afraid of knitting in the round but desire a set of lace place mats for your dining room table, try making rectangular place mats. These work up very quickly and can be made with or without the knitted border. The knitted border is not difficult to make, but I must warn you that it is time-consuming, so if you must have a set of place mats for a dinner party by the end of the week, don't try the knitted border. If you decide to omit the border, you will need approximately one half of the amount of thread indicated in the list of materials.

To make the border, you bind off all but 1 stitch and use this stitch to begin the border. You pick up and work 1 stitch at a time along the four sides of the place mat. You can pick up stitches at random or pick up every other row. Either way, you will produce an attractive scalloped edging.

If you prefer, you can make rectangular place mats without the lacy look. For each one, simply cast on 56 stitches and knit each row until the piece is the required width. The knitted border will be a lovely addition to a plain knitted place mat.

Try to choose a color for your place mats that will match the colors in your dining room. My rectangular place mats were made in orange to match the colors of my modern dining room. If you'd like to have a stripped mat, change the colors every fourth row (or when the pattern is repeated).

SIZE: Approximately 18″ x 13″ (46cm x 33cm).

MATERIALS: Two 100-yard (91.4m) balls Coats & Clark Speed-Cro-Sheen (for each place mat); size 4 knitting needles.

DIRECTIONS: Cast on 56 stitches.
Rows 1, 2 and 3: Knit.
Row 4: Knit 4. *Yarn over, knit 2 together.* Repeat from * to * to the last 4 stitches. Knit 4.
Row 5: Knit 4, purl 48, knit 4.
Row 6: Knit.
Row 7: Knit 4, purl 48, knit 4.
Repeat rows 4, 5, 6 and 7 until the piece measures approximately 16 1/2″ (41.5cm), ending with row 4. Knit 3 rows and bind off loosely, leaving 1 stitch on the needle.
Border: *Yarn over, pick up and knit 1 stitch along the side of the place mat; turn, purl 1, work 7 stitches in the next stitch—*to work 7 stitches in 1 stitch (knit 1, purl 1)*

6 times, knit 1 in the same stitch—purl 1, slip 1 as if to purl; turn, bind off 9 stitches (1 stitch will remain on the right-hand needle).* Repeat from * to * all around the four sides of the place mat. Bind off the last stitch, and fasten off.

FINISHING: Finish following the special suggestions for finishing lace projects in the "Hints on Finishing" section in the appendix. Be sure to pin at frequent intervals around the entire knitted border.

OVAL PLACE MAT

If you own an oval table and have shopped for table-cloths and place mats to grace that table, you undoubtedly have begun to feel like the proverbial stepchild. Round mats, square mats, or rectangular mats are in plentiful supply, but oval mats are always "sold out" or the "we'll be getting them in next week" sign is posted. That's not much help when the dinner party is tomorrow!

Long ago I gave up and started to make my own oval place mats, but I never dreamed of knitting a set. Then one day, in a small shop that calls itself an antique shop but actually sells what my husband refers to as "someone else's old junk," I found an oval knitted doily. Ponce de León wouldn't have been happier if he had found the fountain of youth. I immediately took possession of that oval doily and studied it for several days until I eventually figured out how to make an oval knitted place mat. Here are my instructions.

The entire place mat is made on a circular needle. If you have never used a circular knitting needle before, this is a great introductory project. You start by treating the circular needle as if it were two regular knitting needles, knitting back and forth in rows for 76 rows. It may feel a bit clumsy at first, but as soon as you get the hang of it, you'll discover it really is no different from knitting on two needles. Once you have become accustomed to working with the circular needle, it will seem very natural to pick up stitches along the sides and to begin knitting around and around in rounds.

Of course, you can knit this place mat by working the center on two needles and then switching to a set of double-pointed needles or a circular needle for the border, but I think my way is easier and more fun.

If you find that, after you've worked one place mat, you don't want to make an entire set, use this place mat

as a doily. It will be a rare item because you're not going to find too many patterns for oval knitted doilies.

SIZE: Approximately 14″ x 21″ (35.5cm x 53.5cm).

MATERIALS: Two 100-yard (91.4m) balls red Coats & Clark Speed-Cro-Sheen, one 100-yard (91.4m) ball white Coats & Clark Speed-Cro-Sheen, size 3 circular knitting needle.

Center

DIRECTIONS: With red, cast 15 stitches onto the circular needle. Work back and forth across the needle in rows; do not join or work in rounds.

Row 1: Knit 14. Knit and purl into last stitch. (16 stitches)
Row 2: Knit 15. Knit and purl into last stitch. (17 stitches)
Row 3: Knit 16. Knit and purl into last stitch. (18 stitches)
Row 4: Knit 17. Knit and purl into last stitch. (19 stitches)
Row 5: Knit 18. Knit and purl into last stitch. (20 stitches)
Row 6: Knit 19. Knit and purl into last stitch. (21 stitches)
Row 7: Knit 5, purl 3, (yarn over, knit 1) 5 times, yarn over, purl 3, knit 5. (27 stitches)
Row 8: Knit 5, purl 17, knit 5.
Row 9: Knit.
Row 10: Knit 5, purl 17, knit 5.
Row 11: Knit 5, (purl 2 together) 3 times, (yarn over, knit 1) 5 times, yarn over, (purl 2 together) 3 times, knit 5.
Rows 12, 16, 20, 24, 28, 32, 36, 40, 44, 48, 52, 56, 60 and 64: Knit 5, purl 17, knit 5.
Rows 13, 17, 21, 25, 29, 33, 37, 41, 45, 49, 53, 57, 61 and 65: Knit.
Rows 14, 18, 22, 26, 30, 34, 38, 42, 46, 50, 54, 58, 62 and 66: Knit 5, purl 17, knit 5.
Rows 15, 19, 23, 27, 31, 35, 39, 43, 47, 51, 55, 59, 63 and 67: Knit 5, (purl 2 together) 3 times, (yarn over, knit 1) 5 times, yarn over, (purl 2 together) 3 times, knit 5.
(*Note: You are repeating rows 8, 9, 10 and 11 fourteen times.*)
Row 68: Knit 5, purl 17, knit 5.
Row 69: Knit.
Row 70: Knit 5, purl 17, knit 5.
Row 71: Knit 5, (purl 2 together) 3 times, knit 5, (purl 2 together) 3 times, knit 3, knit 2 together. (20 stitches)
Row 72: Knit 18, knit 2 together. (19 stitches)
Row 73: Knit 17, knit 2 together. (18 stitches)
Row 74: Knit 16, knit 2 together. (17 stitches)
Row 75: Knit 15, knit 2 together. (16 stitches)
Row 76: Knit 14, knit 2 together. (15 stitches)

Border

DIRECTIONS: Knit across the 15 stitches (with the cir-

cular needle). Then, pick up and knit 1 stitch in each of the 38 ridges along one side; knit the 15 stitches across the bottom and the 38 stitches along the other side. There are now 106 stitches on the circular needle; you will now work in rounds rather than back and forth in rows.

NOTE: Always mark the start of each round by placing a safety pin in the first stitch of the round. Move the pin when you reach this stitch and replace it in the new stitch just formed.

Round 1: *(Knit and purl in the stitch) 12 times, knit 29, (knit and purl in the stitch) 12 times.* Repeat from * to * around the round. (154 stitches)
Round 2: *Purl 3, (yarn over, knit 1) 5 times, yarn over, purl 3.* Repeat from * to * around the round. (238 stitches)
Rounds 3, 4 and 5: Knit.
Round 6: *(Purl 2 together) 3 times, (yarn over, knit 1) 5 times, yarn over, (purl 2 together) 3 times.* Repeat from * to * around the round. (238 stitches)
Rounds 7, 8 and 9: Knit.
Round 10: *(Purl 2 together) 3 times, (yarn over, knit 1) 5 times, yarn over, (purl 2 together) 3 times.* Repeat from * to * around the round. (238 stitches)
Rounds 11, 12 and 13: Knit.
Round 14: *(Purl 2 together) 3 times, (yarn over, knit 1) 5 times, yarn over, (purl 2 together) 3 times.* Repeat from * to * around the round. (238 stitches)
Rounds 15, 16 and 17: Knit.
Round 18: *(Purl 2 together) 3 times, (yarn over, knit 1) 5 times, yarn over, (purl 2 together) 3 times.* Repeat from * to * around the round. (238 stitches)
Rounds 19, 20 and 21: Knit.
Round 22: *(Purl 2 together) 3 times, (yarn over, knit 1) 5 times, yarn over, (purl 2 together) 3 times.* Repeat from * to * around the round. (238 stitches)
Rounds 23, 24 and 25: Knit.
Round 26: Cut red thread; attach white and work with white for the rest of the pattern. *(Purl 2 together) 2 times, (yarn over, knit 1) 9 times, yarn over, (purl 2 together) 2 times.* Repeat from * to * around the round. (322 stitches)
Round 27: Knit.
Rounds 28, 29 and 30: Purl.
Round 31: Knit 1. *Knit 2 together, yarn over, knit 2 together; turn, purl 1, work 5 stitches in the next stitch— *to work 5 stitches in 1 stitch (knit 1, purl 1) 2 times, knit 1 in the same stitch*—purl 1, slip 1 as if to purl; turn, bind off 7 stitches (1 stitch will remain on the right-hand needle).* Repeat from * to * around the round to the last 5 stitches. Knit 3 together, yarn over, knit 2 together; turn, purl 1, work 5 stitches in the next stitch, purl 1, slip 1 as if to purl; turn, bind off the remaining stitches. Fasten off.

FINISHING: Finish following the special suggestions for finishing lace projects in the "Hints on Finishing" section in the appendix. Be sure to pin at frequent intervals around the entire knitted border.

THE WORLD'S EASIEST LACE TABLECLOTH

I have known many wonderful ladies who spent the better part of a lifetime making a lace tablecloth for one of those huge dining room tables that once graced our homes. If you are fortunate enough to own one of these handmade lace cloths, hang on to it and treat it kindly because such cloths are rapidly becoming collectors' items. They are commanding fantastic prices in antique-type shops. I suppose if you buy an old table, you will need an old lace tablecloth to cover it.

I don't own a huge dining room table. My dining room boasts a small round table that can be opened, and with the addition of some leaves it magically turns into a large oval table. Although I have always had the secret desire to cover the table with a lace tablecloth, I've never had the nerve to make one. I was always afraid of all the washing, blocking and ironing that I remember a lace tablecloth required. And I—like most modern women—am too busy to devote half a lifetime to making a lace tablecloth. If I were to make a lace tablecloth, no more than a week's knitting should be required and that must be completed in front of the TV.

So I invented "The World's Easiest Lace Tablecloth". The entire cloth is made with a knit stitch, a yarn over, and a knit 1 or a knit 2 together. No fancy stitches; no elaborate instructions that require you to keep counting stitches to make certain you haven't lost any!

This tablecloth will require no elaborate blocking. Simply wash it, roll it in a Turkish towel to remove some of the moisture and then let it dry right on the table. Of course, you have to be certain that the finish on your table is impervious to moisture. If you are not certain, it is better to assume that the table's finish won't be able to take the wet cloth and to protect your table in the following manner. If you have pads for your table, place the pads on the table and cover the pads with some heavy paper. (If you do not have pads, place the heavy paper directly on the table.) Cover the paper with a large piece of plastic. This can be a plastic tablecloth, an old shower curtain, or an inexpensive drop cloth, which can be purchased at a paint or variety store. After the tablecloth has dried, it may require a little touch up with a steam iron, especially along the parts that hang down the sides of the table and around the knitted border. The tablecloth is now ready for use!

The instructions are for a 36''-round table (91.5cm) because that's the size of my own table, and because it is about as large a cloth as I think anyone can do in a week. If you want to make the tablecloth large enough to fit a 48''-round table (122cm), keep working to row 164, knitting around the odd rounds and working the yarn over, knit 2 together pattern on the even rounds. A 54''-table (137cm) will require your working 182 rows, knitting the odd rounds and working the yarn over, knit 2 together pattern on the even rounds. Do not work any increase.

You *can* keep knitting until you have a tablecloth that will fit King Arthur's Round Table, but let's be realistic. By the time you complete the 36'', the 48'' or the 54'' tablecloth you will have 576 stitches on your needle. If you keep knitting, the next time you increase (about row 197) you will have 1,152 stitches on the needle. It will take you a week just to get around one round! The tablecloth is going to end up in that pile of unfinished projects that "I'm going to get to when I get myself organized" or ". . . when I retire." The first rule for being a successful knitter is never to undertake a project that is going to be larger than what you can comfortably finish before getting bored.

The tablecloth is worked on a circular needle. If you are lucky enough to live in a town that still has one of those good old-fashioned knitting shops, or if you have a good craft supply shop nearby, you may be able to get circular needles in various lengths. You can begin with a short needle and then move on to longer and longer needles as stitches are added. You can do this entire tablecloth, however, on a 24'' circular needle, which will hold all of the stitches even if they are a bit crowded. Just as with a doily, you will have to begin knitting with four double-pointed needles. You must struggle along with them until you get to about the thirteenth round, when you will be able to move onto the circular needle. If you've never worked with a circular needle or knitted in the round before, read the special instructions given in the appendix.

Note that the entire tablecloth is worked with two strands of thread. While it is possible to work with a single strand, I find that the heavier weight of the two strands makes the cloth hang better and may very well be the reason why blocking is no problem.

SIZE: Will fit 36''-round table (91.5cm).

MATERIALS: Ten 218-yard (200m) balls DMC Brilliant Crochet Cotton, size 11 double-pointed knitting needles (set of four), size 11 circular knitting needle.

NOTE: Always mark the start of each round by placing a safety pin in the first stitch of the round. Move the pin when you reach this stitch and replace it in the new stitch just formed.

DIRECTIONS: Working with two strands, cast 9 stitches onto one double-pointed needle. Divide the stitches evenly onto three needles; join, being careful not to twist the stitches.

Round 1: Knit.
Round 2: *Yarn over, knit 1.* Repeat from * to * around the round. (18 stitches)
Round 3: Knit.
Round 4: *Yarn over, knit 2 together.* Repeat from * to * around the round.
Round 5: Knit.
Round 6: *Yarn over, knit 1.* Repeat from * to * around the round. (36 stitches)
Rounds 7, 9, 11 and 12: Knit.
Rounds 8 and 10: *Yarn over, knit 2 together.* Repeat from * to * around the round.
Round 13: *Yarn over, knit 1.* Repeat from * to * around the round. (72 stitches)
Rounds 14, 16, 18, 20, 22, 24 and 25: Knit.
Rounds 15, 17, 19, 21 and 23: *Yarn over, knit 2 together.* Repeat from * to * around the round.
Round 26: *Yarn over, knit 1.* Repeat from * to * around the round. (144 stitches)
Rounds 27, 29, 31, 33, 35, 37, 39, 41, 43, 45, 47, 49 and 50: Knit.
Rounds 28, 30, 32, 34, 36, 38, 40, 42, 44, 46 and 48: *Yarn over, knit 2 together.* Repeat from * to * around the round.
Round 51: *Yarn over, knit 1.* Repeat from * to * around the round. (288 stitches)
Rounds 52, 54, 56, 58, 60, 62, 64, 66, 68, 70, 72, 74, 76, 78, 80, 82, 84, 86, 88, 90, 92, 94, 96, 98 and 99: Knit.
Rounds 53, 55, 57, 59, 61, 63, 65, 67, 69, 71, 73, 75, 77, 79, 81, 83, 85, 87, 89, 91, 93, 95 and 97: *Yarn over, knit 1.* Repeat from * to * around the round.
Round 100: *Yarn over, knit 1.* Repeat from * to * around the round. (576 stitches)
Rounds 101, 103, 105, 107, 109, 111, 113, 115, 117, 119 and 121: Knit.
Rounds 102, 104, 106, 108, 110, 112, 114, 116, 118 and 120: *Yarn over, knit 2 together.* Repeat from * to * around the round.
Round 122: Knit 1. *Knit 2 together, yarn over, knit 2 together; turn, purl 1, work 5 stitches in the next stitch— *to work 5 stitches in 1 stitch (knit 1, purl 1) 2 times, knit 1 in the same stitch*—purl 1, slip 1 as if to purl; turn, bind off 7 stitches (1 stitch will remain on the right-hand needle).* Repeat from * to * around the round to the last 3 stitches. Knit 2 together, yarn over, knit 1; turn, purl 1, work 5 stitches in the next stitch, purl 1, slip 1 as if to purl; turn, bind off the remaining 7 stitches and fasten off.

FINISHING: Wash the tablecloth, roll it in a Turkish towel to remove some of the moisture. Dry it on the table, following the instructions on page 24 for protecting your table. A little touch up with a steam iron, especially along the border may be necessary.

FRUIT BASKET

Not only did my mother and her friends never leave a dining room table uncovered, but they always had to place some piece of "art" on the lace tablecloth. Most of the time it was a bowl filled with fruit. During most of the year, when the table sat by itself in lonely exile in the cold dining room, the fruit was of the artificial variety. When the dining room table was in use during holiday festivities, the fruit bowl was filled with the most enticing and colorful variety of real fruit, which rivaled the artificial ones in perfection and beauty.

My mother's guests knew the difference between the regular variety of fruits (the artificial ones) and the holiday type (the real ones), but I remember that one year my brother was able to fool me into taking a big bite into a wax apple. That tooth-marked apple remained for years, a silent reminder of my brother's cleverness, or rather, of my stupidity.

I still don't think a dining room table is complete unless it has a fruit bowl, but I want fresh fruit in my fruit bowl! So instead of telling you how to knit artificial fruit, here are instructions for making a fruit basket. If you don't want to use it for fruit, the basket will serve many other purposes. You can deposit balls of yarn, candy, Easter eggs, perfume bottles, or hairpins in it. You can even use it to hold a casserole during a buffet dinner.

The basket is made by knitting a circular piece, stiffening it with sugar, and then shaping it over a round bowl. This technique of using sugar to stiffen knitting is a very old one. As a girl I recall that people made all sorts of fancy baskets with bits of crochet and sugar. That technique has gone out of style during the past thirty years, but it's lots of fun.

The circular piece is made just like a round doily. You begin in the center on four double-pointed needles. See the appendix for suggestions on knitting in the round.

SIZE: Approximately 6 1/2'' in diameter (16.5 cm).

MATERIALS: One 218-yard (200m) ball DMC Brilliant Crochet Cotton, size 4 double-pointed knitting needles (set of four), size 11 circular knitting needle, bowl measuring 6 1/2'' (16.5 cm) in diameter and at least 4'' (10cm) high, sugar, water.

NOTE: Always mark the start of each round by placing a safety pin in the first stitch of the round. Move the pin when you reach this stitch and replace it in the new stitch just formed.

Bottom of Basket

DIRECTIONS: Cast 6 stitches onto one double-pointed needle. Divide the stitches evenly onto three needles; join, being careful not to twist the stitches.

Round 1: Knit.

Round 2: *Knit 1, yarn over.* Repeat from * to * around the round. (12 stitches)

Round 3: *Knit into the front and the back of the stitch, yarn over, knit into the front and the back of the stitch, yarn over.* Repeat from * to * around the round. (36 stitches)

Round 4: Knit.

Round 5: *Knit 1, yarn over, knit 5, yarn over.* Repeat from * to * around the round. (48 stitches)

Round 6: Knit.

Round 7: *Knit 1, yarn over, knit 7, yarn over.* Repeat from * to * around the round. (60 stitches)

Round 8: Knit.

Round 9: *Knit 1, yarn over, knit 9, yarn over.* Repeat from * to * around the round. (72 stitches)

Round 10: Knit.

Round 11: *Knit 1, yarn over, knit 11, yarn over.* Repeat from * to * around the round. (84 stitches)

Round 12: Knit.

Round 13: *Knit 1, (yarn over, knit 2 together) 3 times, yarn over, knit 1, (yarn over, slip 1, knit 1, pass the slip stitch over the knit stitch) 3 times, yarn over.* Repeat from * to * around the round. (96 stitches)

Round 14: Knit.

Round 15: *Knit 1, (yarn over, knit 2 together) 3 times, yarn over, knit 3, (yarn over, slip 1 as if to purl, knit 1, pass the slip stitch over the knit stitch) 3 times, yarn over.* Repeat from * to * around the round. (108 stitches)

Round 16: Knit.

Round 17: *Knit 1, (yarn over, knit 2 together) 4 times, yarn over, knit 1, (yarn over, slip 1 as if to purl, knit 1, pass the slip stitch over the knit stitch) 4 times, yarn over.* Repeat from * to * around the round. (120 stitches)

Round 18: Knit.

Round 19: *Yarn over, knit 1, (yarn over, knit 2 together) 4 times, yarn over, knit 3 together, (yarn over, slip 1 as if to purl, knit 1, pass the slip stitch over the knit stitch) 4 times.* Repeat from * to * around the round. (120 stitches)

Round 20: Knit.

Round 21: *Yarn over, knit 3, yarn over, slip 1 as if to purl, knit 1, pass the slip stitch over the knit stitch, yarn over, knit 3 together, yarn over, knit 2 together, yarn over, knit 3, yarn over, slip 1 as if to purl, knit 1, pass the slip stitch over the knit stitch, yarn over, knit 3 together, yarn over, knit 2 together.* Repeat from * to * around the round. (120 stitches)

Round 22: Knit.

Sides of Basket

DIRECTIONS: Continue working the stitches on the circular needle.

Round 1: *Yarn over, knit 5, yarn over, slip 1 as if to purl, knit 1, pass the slip stitch over the knit stitch, knit 1, knit 2 together.* Repeat from * to * around the round. (120 stitches)

Round 2: Knit.

Round 3: *Yarn over, knit 7, yarn over, knit 3 together.* Repeat from * to * around the round. (120 stitches)

Round 4: Knit.

Round 5: *Knit 5, (yarn over) 4 times, knit 5.* Repeat from * to * around the round. (168 stitches)

Round 6: *Knit 5, work 9 stitches in the first yarn over—*to work 9 stitches in 1 stitch (knit 1, purl 1) 4 times, knit 1 in the same stitch*—let the 3 other yarn overs slip off the left-hand needle, knit 5.* Repeat from * to * around the round. (228 stitches)

Round 7: *Knit 5, yarn over, knit 9, yarn over, knit 5.* Repeat from * to * around the round. (252 stitches)

Round 8: Knit.

Round 9: *Knit 5, yarn over, knit 11, yarn over, knit 5.* Repeat from * to * around the round. (276 stitches)

Round 10: Knit.

Round 11: *Knit 3, (knit 2 together, yarn over) 4 times, knit 1, (yarn over, slip 1 as if to purl, knit 1, pass the slip stitch over the knit stitch) 4 times, knit 3.* Repeat from * to * around the round. (276 stitches)

Round 12: Knit.

Round 13: *Knit 2, (knit 2 together, yarn over) 4 times, knit 3, (yarn over, slip 1 as if to purl, knit 1, pass the slip stitch over the knit stitch) 4 times, knit 2.* Repeat from * to * around the round. (276 stitches)

Round 14: Knit.

Round 15: *Knit 1, (knit 2 together, yarn over) 5 times, work 3 stitches in the next stitch—*to work 3 stitches in 1 stitch, knit 1, purl 1, knit 1 in the same stitch*—(yarn over, slip 1 as if to purl, knit 1, pass the slip stitch over the knit stitch) 5 times, knit 1.* Repeat from * to * around the round. (300 stitches)

Round 16: Knit.

Round 17: *(Knit 2 together, yarn over) 5 times, knit 5, (yarn over, slip 1 as if to purl, knit 1, pass the slip stitch over the knit stitch) 5 times.* Repeat from * to * around the round. (300 stitches)

Round 18: Knit. Bind off loosely.

FINISHING: Wash and pin into shape, making certain that all twelve points have been pulled out. Let dry. Mix 1/3 cup of sugar with 4 tablespoons of water until the sugar has started to dissolve. Heat the solution on the stove until the sugar is completely dissolved. Remove the solution from the heat and soak the knitting in the solution until it is completely wet and most of the sugar water has been absorbed. Let cool slightly. Wring out the knitting and shape it over the inverted bowl. Place the bowl and the knitting in a warm place to dry. This may take several days. I like to start the drying process by placing the knitting over the inverted bowl in the oven for a few minutes. Heat the oven to about 350°F, turn off the heat and place the knitting on the bowl on the middle shelf, leaving the door open. Don't be dismayed, by the way, if the knitting starts to change color during the drying process; the original color will return. When the knitting is completely dry, remove it from the bowl.

3.

THE KITCHEN

I love kitchens! I always have! A kitchen should be a large room with a big table sitting in the center of it. The table rightfully deserves to be the center of life in the household, beckoning the family members to come and do everything from reading the newspaper and doing homework to shelling peas. A kitchen should smell of mysterious spices, and huge sheets of steam should bellow forth from singing pots perched happily on the stove—a center of the universe.

Of course, I imagine those kitchens in other people's houses. I'm much too busy following a career or reading the latest book on women's liberation to have a real kitchen. I like to cook, but not the daily meat and potato dishes. I like to make coq au vin, vichyssoise or a veal ragout about once a month, enjoying every minute of peeling, slicing, coring and whatever else has to be done. In between, however, I'd prefer eating out. There's no room for that large table in my kitchen; it's strictly eat and run—like an at-home McDonald's. I prefer it this way.

But there are moments when I get little twinges of guilt, especially when I think that my own daughters are growing up without knowing what a "real" kitchen should look like. When I feel those twinges start, I take two knitting needles and make plans to call Betty Friedan or Gloria Steinem in the morning. My daughters are going to have to learn about kitchens from watching television.

An analyst would most probably say that anyone who *knits* for her kitchen is trying to rid herself of guilt feelings. That might very well be true; perhaps in knitting projects for the kitchen I am subconsciously reaching for that big, old-fashioned kitchen like the one in which I did my homework. After all, most "normal" people would stand in the middle of the kitchen and say, "No room for knitted things here!" But to an inveterate knitter like me, the kitchen cannot escape. After all, a kitchen deserves to be knitted for; underneath it all, it's a great room—even if I do mistreat it.

In this chapter you are going to find some things that I've made for my kitchen, but there are a number of other projects in this book that might be suitable for your kitchen, depending upon the type you have. If you have a very formal kitchen with cabinets that are actually expensive pieces of furniture hung on the walls, then why not knit the lace tablecloth or the luncheon set found in chapter 2. Many of the projects in the chapter on dens and family rooms might be suitable for an informal kitchen. The lace edgings in chapter 9 would make lovely shelf trimmings for your kitchen cabinets, and the plant holders in the chapter on sun porches might look great in your kitchen windows. If you really want to knit for your kitchen, just browse through this book, and you'll find many projects to put into the kitchen.

POT HOLDERS AND RACK

There are always crowds of people working in my kitchen. I suspect it is self-defense that has forced my husband and daughters into the kitchen. Because I only like to cook the most elaborate food, they have to prepare the simple kinds of food that most people eat. I can spend hours preparing a perfect beef Wellington, but after almost a quarter of a century in the kitchen I still find it difficult to get the potatoes to join the string beans and the meat at the proper time.

Everyone in our family pitches in to help prepare dinner. We are a collection of specialists; the salad maker does not infringe upon the territory of the potato chef. It doesn't matter if one of the girls is away for six months; the day she comes home, she's back in the kitchen, acting out our little dinner-time ballet without missing a step. Over the years we've learned to synchronize our watches so that all parts of the meal are prepared at the right time.

Although we never get into each other's way, pot holders always seem to disappear just at the crucial moment when someone must remove a hot pot from the stove or court disaster. The available pot holders are always in someone else's hands. That's why I am constantly making pot holders for my kitchen.

This project calls for three pot holders and a rack from which to hang them. The pot holders and the rack are made in matching colors, but you can use any scraps of four-ply knitting worsted to make a spare pot holder. Since a pot holder is going to be used in the kitchen, it is important to use a thread that will not burn or catch fire easily. Most synthetics will melt from the heat even if the advertising copy insists that they will not catch fire. Make sure of your thread before you start the project. Actually, the best type to use would be a wool yarn; it won't melt and will withstand quite a bit of heat before burning. Wool may present some problems in washing and drying in that you may not be able to just pop it into the washing machine and the dryer.

The pot holders and the rack are made by a process called double knitting. This produces a tubular piece that is the same on both sides and is joined at the bottom, or cast-on, edge. The stitch can be used to create a double thickness for a flat piece for which extra insulation is desired, such as the pot holders or a scarf; or it can be used to make a tubular piece that is to be filled, such as the rack or a pillow cover. It can also be used to make a tubular piece that is to be left open, such as a purse. The only difference is in the binding off. To bind off a purse or other piece that will have an opening, you slip every other stitch onto a spare needle and bind off the stitches on the first needle, then turn the work and bind off the stitches on the spare needle. For a project that will be filled, such as the rack or a pillow cover, slip every other stitch onto another needle, open the knitting, insert the necessary filling material between the two pieces of knitting, and then bind off, working 2 stitches together each time, one from the front needle and one from the back. If you are just making a flat piece with double thickness, such as the pot holders, you merely bind off as usual, working 2 stitches together each time instead of one.

SIZE: Pot holders: approximately 6'' (15cm) square. Rack: approximately 11'' x 2'' (28cm) x 5cm).

MATERIALS: 2 ounces red four-ply knitting worsted, 2 ounces blue four-ply knitting worsted, 2 ounces yellow four-ply knitting worsted, size 7 knitting needles, size 3 double-pointed knitting needles (set of two), 11'' x 2'' (28cm x 5cm) scrap of 3/8'' (10mm) plywood, three small cup hooks.

RED POT HOLDER

DIRECTIONS: With red, cast on 44 stitches as tightly as possible.

Rows 1 and 2: *Knit 1, wool forward, slip 1 as if to purl, purl 1, slip 1 as if to purl, wool back.* Repeat from * to * across the row.

Rows 3 and 4: *Purl 1, slip 1 as if to purl, wool back, knit 1, wool forward, slip 1 as if to purl.* Repeat from * to * across the row.

Repeat these 4 rows until the piece is a square, approximately 6'' (15cm). Bind off as usual, working 2 stitches together each time instead of only one, until 2 stitches remain on the needle. Place these 2 stitches onto a double-pointed needle.

Loop: *Knit 2. *Do not turn.* Slide the stitches to the other end of the double-pointed needle.* Repeat from * to * until the loop measures approximately 3'' (7.6cm). (To keep the cord from curling as you work, pull on the cord before knitting the stitch.) Attach the loose end of the loop to the pot holder to make a loop.

YELLOW POT HOLDER

DIRECTIONS: With yellow, cast on 44 stitches as tightly as possible. Follow instructions for Red Pot Holder.

BLUE POT HOLDER

DIRECTIONS: With blue, cast on 44 stitches as tightly as possible. Follow instructions for Red Pot Holder.

RACK

DIRECTIONS: With red, cast on 16 stitches.

Rows 1 and 2: *Knit 1, wool forward, slip 1 as if to purl, purl 1, slip 1 as if to purl, wool back.* Repeat from * to * across the row.

Rows 3 and 4: *Purl 1, slip 1 as if to purl, wool back, knit 1, wool forward, slip 1 as if to purl.* Repeat from * to * across the row.

Repeat these 4 rows until the piece measures 3 1/2'' (9cm). Cut red, attach yellow and repeat the 4 rows until the piece measures 7'' (18cm). Cut yellow, attach blue and repeat the 4 rows until the piece measures 10 1/2'' (27cm). Slip every other stitch onto a spare needle to create a tubular piece. Open the knitting and insert the piece of wood. Bind off by working 2 stitches together (one from the front needle and one from the back needle).

CORD

DIRECTIONS: With yellow, cast 3 stitches onto a double-pointed needle. *Knit 3. *Do not turn.* Slide the stitches to the other end of the double-pointed needle.* Repeat from * to * until the cord measures approximately 20'' (51cm). (To keep the cord from curling as you work, pull on the cord before knitting the stitches.) Bind off in the usual manner.

FINISHING: Join the cord to the rack. Screw cup hooks into the rack, spacing them as shown in the photograph.

VEGETABLE BAGS

Before the advent of plastic containers, onions, potatoes, carrots and other vegetables were often sold in string bags. When you brought these vegetables home from the market, you could store them in the string bags, which allowed air to circulate so that the vegetables would not rot too soon. In those big kitchens I only dare dream about now, women were not ashamed to leave their string bags laden with vegetables in full view—a privilege not afforded by the plastic bags currently used by the stores. If you notice that your potatoes and onions seem to be rotting sooner than they should, don't blame it on the new breed of vegetables. A plastic bag won't let your vegetables breathe, so they start to rot. Knitted vegetables bags are not only decorative elements in your kitchen, they also keep your vegetables fresh much longer.

In Europe, string shopping bags are very popular. You fold up the string bag in your purse, and then as you go from shop to shop you fill it with your purchases. The string bag expands with each purchase so that something that took up very little space on the trip to the market can hold a lot of groceries on the trip home. Even if you don't want to use one for carrying groceries, a string bag can be handy for that Saturday afternoon when you decide to browse in your favorite boutiques.

Knitted bags are really quite simple to make. The ones shown here were made with crochet cotton, but the same instructions can be used to make bags out of string, butcher's twine, macrame cord and even yarn.

Vegetable Bag as a Shopping Purse

You have to begin working on a set of double-pointed needles. By the time you reach round 12, you can switch to a circular needle. (Of course, you can continue working on the four double-pointed needles, but the circular needle is a lot safer and more fun.) When you get to the fiftieth round, you knit onto a smaller circular needle to make the band across the top of the bag. Letters knitted into the band spell out the contents of the bag. The letters are worked with a second color following a chart. If you prefer, you can knit a plain band and then embroider in the letters after you finish knitting the bag. For the final two rounds of band, you return to the larger circular needle. Then, to make the handles, you work back and forth in rows on a pair of straight knitting needles or on the circular needle, whichever you prefer. See the appendix for hints on knitting in the round.

MATERIALS: Four 100-yard (91.5m) balls white Coats & Clark Speed-Cro-Sheen, one 100-yard (91.5m) ball (or small amount left over from another project) red Coats & Clark Speed-Cro-Sheen, size 11 double-pointed knitting needles (set of four), size 11 circular knitting needle, size 11 straight knitting needles (optional), size 4 circular knitting needle, stitch holder.

NOTE: Always mark the start of each round by placing a safety pin in the first stitch of the round. Move the pin when you reach this stitch and replace it in the new stitch just formed.

Body

DIRECTIONS: With white, cast 9 stitches onto one double-pointed needle. Divide the stitches evenly onto three needles; join, being careful not to twist the stitches.
Round 1: Knit.
Round 2: *Yarn over, knit 1.* Repeat from * to * around the round. (18 stitches)
Round 3: Knit.
Round 4: *Yarn over, knit 2 together.* Repeat from * to * around the round.
Round 5: Knit.
Round 6: *Yarn over, knit 1.* Repeat from * to * around the round. (36 stitches)
Round 7: Knit.
Round 8: *Yarn over, knit 2 together.* Repeat from * to * around the round.
Round 9: Knit.
Round 10: *Yarn over, knit 2 together.* Repeat from * to * around the round.
Round 11: Knit.

Round 12: *Yarn over, knit 1.* Repeat from * to * around the round. (72 stitches)

Rounds 13, 15, 17, 19, 21 and 23: Knit.

Rounds 14, 16, 18, 20 and 22: *Yarn over, knit 2 together.* Repeat from * to * around the round.

Round 24: *(Yarn over, knit 1) 2 times, yarn over, knit 2 together.* Repeat from * to * around the round. (108 stitches)

Rounds 25, 27, 29, 31, 33, 35, 37, 39, 41, 43, 45, 47 and 49: Knit.

Rounds 26, 28, 30, 32, 34, 36, 38, 40, 42, 44, 46 and 48: *Yarn over, knit 2 together.* Repeat from * to * around the round.

Round 50: Knit onto the size 4 circular needle. *Yarn over, knit 2 together, (yarn over, knit 1) 4 times.* Repeat from * to * around the round to the last 6 stitches. (Yarn over, knit 2 together) 3 times. (176 stitches)

Rounds 51, 52 and 53: Knit.

Rounds 54, 55, 56, 57, 58, 59 and 60: Knit. Work in one color (white) if you wish to add embroidered letters after the bag has been completed. To knit the letters directly into the band, attach red and follow the lettering chart for "onions" or "potatoes," stranding the red thread as you work. (See the appendix for instructions on working with two colors).

Rounds 61 and 62: Knit.

Round 63: Knit onto size 11 circular needle. (Knit 2 together) 4 times. *(Knit 2 together) 2 times, (knit 2 together, knit 1) 4 times.* Repeat from * to * around the round to the last 8 stitches. (Knit 2 together) 4 times. (108 stitches)

Round 64: *Yarn over, knit 2 together.* Repeat from * to * around the round.

Round 65: Knit.

Round 66: *Yarn over, knit 2 together.* Repeat from * to * around the round.

Handles

DIRECTIONS: With a size 11 knitting needle, knit across 54 stitches and place these on a stitch holder. Knit across the last 54 stitches. You now work back and forth in rows instead of in rounds.

Row 1: Purl 2 together, purl 50, purl 2 togehter. (52 stitches)

Row 2: Knit 2 together. *Yarn over, knit 2 together.* Repeat from * to * across the row to the last 2 stitches. Knit 2 together.

Row 3: Purl.

Rows 4, 6, 8, 10, 12, 14, 16, 18, 20, 22, 24, 26, 28, 30, 32, 34, 36 and 38: Repeat row 2 until 14 stitches remain on the needle.

Rows 5, 7, 9, 11, 13, 15, 17, 19, 21, 23, 25, 27, 29, 31, 33, 35, 37 and 39: Repeat row 3.

Row 40: (Knit 2 together) 7 times. (7 stitches)

Row 41: (Knit 2 together) 3 times, knit 1. (4 stitches)

Row 42: (Knit 2 together) 2 times. (2 stitches)

Bind off the remaining 2 stitches.

To make the second handle, attach thread to the stitches on the stitch holder and repeat the instructions.

FINISHING: Join the two handle sections at the top. If you have made a plain band, you can embroider the letters spelling out the contents of the bag. To do this, you follow the chart for "onions" or "potatoes" and actually cover the original stockinette stitch with a new color.

Embroidery on Stockinette Stitch

Thread a large-eyed tapestry needle with the contrasting color. From the back of the bag, put the needle into the base of the stitch that you wish to cover. Pass the needle behind the 2 threads forming the stitch and then down again into the base of the stitch from the front. Continue until the pattern has been worked. The bag will probably require no finishing other than weaving in the loose ends of thread, following the instructions in the "Hints on Finishing" section of the appendix.

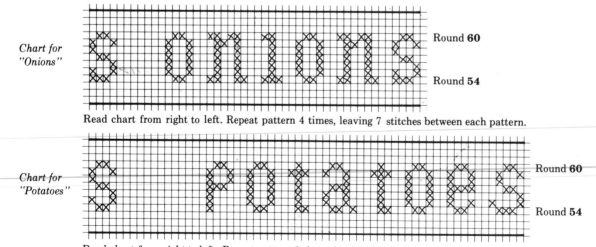

Chart for "Onions"

Round **60**

Round **54**

Read chart from right to left. Repeat pattern 4 times, leaving 7 stitches between each pattern.

Chart for "Potatoes"

Round **60**

Round **54**

Read chart from right to left. Repeat pattern 3 times, leaving 12 stitches between first and second pattern and 13 stitches between the others.

4.

THE DEN

Library, study or den—call it what you will, this room is always masculine! Perhaps the reading of old novels, in which the males of the family would retreat into this lair to sip their brandy, smoke their pipes and cigars (to keep the odor away from the living room draperies, no doubt) and talk about topics that might be too delicate for ladies' ears, has left its mark upon me. A den was always what the name implied: a dark room with a great desk and huge leather furniture, a room into which females entered only upon invitation.

Of course, we never had a room like that in our house. My father didn't smoke cigars, but I think if he had, he would have had to smoke them outdoors, behind the house. It just wasn't part of our lifestyle for my father to have a special room. I remember a friend whose father did have a den. Occasionally we would enter to find a sharpened pencil or a particular book. We weren't permitted to touch the material on his desk, and we hardly dared breath for fear that we might disturb the dust that had settled.

I still tend to think of dens as masculine enclaves although, at some point, the introduction of television opened the doors and let the ladies in. After the TV set had completely destroyed the American living room, the decorators told us that we had made a mistake in the first place and that the den was the obvious place for the TV set. Move over dad, the TV set is going into the den, and you're going to have to share your room with the whole family.

Once we changed its use, the den was no longer a place for dad to run and hide in. Instead, it became an informal living room, and we renamed it the "family room." We can now do almost anything in the family room: smoke cigars, eat limburger cheese, watch Monday-night football, and put our shoes on the furniture. Everything in the family room is designed for casual living, leaving everything in the living room for formal occasions. Most of our dads are perfectly happy to stay in the family room because, after all, that's where the TV set is.

In this chapter you'll find some of the things that I've made for my den/family room. I've included some knitted rugs because rather than wall-to-wall carpeting, in our family room we have wide-planked wood flooring, which some smooth talking salesman told me would be a lot easier to keep clean than carpeting. (I forgot that a wood floor would need to be waxed and highly polished to look good, while carpeting simply needs vacuuming.) I've also included one afghan in this chapter. Actually no one ever curls up on the sofa or in a chair in our den without covering himself with an afghan. The "Ripple Afghan" is the one we keep in this room, but someone is always dashing into the living room to get "Miss Marx's Afghan Done One Better" or a "Warm-all."

If you do a lot of eating in your den, you might want to look at the place mats in chapter 2, "The Dining Room." If yours is a really informal room, check chapter 5, "The Sun Porch," for other projects that you might enjoy in your den or family room.

36 THE DEN

RIPPLE AFGHAN

Hidden somewhere in everyone's childhood memories there has to be a "Ripple Afghan." Remember lying on the couch recuperating from a bout with some childhood disease like measles, scarlet fever or chicken pox (those were the days before one shot kept you free forever from missing school)? There was always a ripple afghan across your feet or over your shoulders as you lay there with the shades drawn so that you could try to sleep, while the noises of yor healthy friends running up and down outside made any kind of rest impossible. For years the ripple afghan has been the world's most popular afghan; you must have seen at least one in your lifetime.

Most ripple afghans are made with a crochet hook, but making one with knitting needles is really quite simple to do. Actually, the pattern consists of only two different rows, which are worked alternately. One row is just a purl row, and the other row contains increases and decreases to give the scallop effect. You decrease the same number of stitches that you increase so you always end up with the same number of stitches.

The rippling effect in the afghan is always highlighted by using different shades of the same color and moving from dark to light, from dark to light. In this afghan, I used different shades of blue,starting with a very dark blue, and moving to a medium blue, a light blue, and a very light blue that is almost white. You work 6 rows of the pattern for each color (3 purl rows and 3 increase-decrease rows). You must begin the afghan with 2 rows of plain knitting so that the first color starts with only 4 rows of the pattern.

This afghan works up very quickly because you use a bulky yarn and very large needles. You can work with a less bulky yarn and thinner needles, but you will have to cast on more stitches and work more rows. For those traditionalists who like a gauge, you will find that approximately 3″ (7.5cm) will equal 10 stitches and 6 rows will equal 2″ (5cm). You can make your own gauge depending upon the type of yarn you use and the desired length and width of the afghan.

SIZE: Approximately 47″ x 90″ (119.5cm x 228.5cm).

MATERIALS: 11 ounces very dark blue Aunt Lydia's Heavy Rug Yarn, 11 ounces medium blue Aunt Lydia's Heavy Rug Yarn, 11 ounces light blue Aunt Lydia's Heavy Rug Yarn, 11 ounces very light blue Aunt Lydia's Heavy Rug Yarn, size 11 knitting needles.

PATTERN:
Row 1: *Knit 1. With the point of the right-hand needle behind the left needle, insert the right needle through the loop below the next stitch (the stitch of the previous row) and draw the yarn through to form a stitch, knit the original stitch on the left-hand needle, knit 3, knit 3 together, knit 3. With the point of the right-hand needle behind the left needle, insert the right needle through the loop below the next stitch (the stitch of the previous row) and draw the yarn through to form a stitch, knit the original stitch on the left-hand needle.* Repeat from * to * across the row to the last stitch. Knit 1.
Row 2: Purl.

DIRECTIONS: With very dark blue, cast on 157 stitches very loosely.
Very dark blue: Knit 2 rows. Work 4 rows of the pattern. *NOTE: On repeats of this color, work 6 rows of the pattern.*
Medium blue: Work 6 rows of the pattern.
Light blue: Work 6 rows of the pattern.
Very light blue: Work 6 rows of the pattern.
Repeat these stripes 10 more times (or until the afghan is the desired length), working 6 rows of the pattern for each color.
Very dark blue: Work 4 rows of the pattern. Purl 1 row and bind off very loosely.

FINISHING: Finish following the suggestions in the "Hints on Finishing" section in the appendix. Block carefully to retain the scallops across the top.

MY CHAIR

I'm sure that many of you have at some time or another owned a chair like "My Chair." It should have been retired many years ago but, somehow, I can't part with it. "My Chair" came from my very first apartment, and then it was part of my dowry when I got married. I nursed my newborn babies in it. I sat in that chair while we drew up the plans for our first house. "When are you going to throw that old thing out?" my husband kept asking. But a chair like that you just don't consign to the trash heap. No matter that the original design wasn't that great to begin with. No matter that the upholstery was stained or that most of the wood had been scratched by generations of cats and dogs. It was *my* chair.

In order not to embarrass the rest of my family, who saw the chair as the piece of junk it probably was, I took to throwing a knitted afghan over the chair. Then, one day it came to me in a flash. Since the knitted afghan not only looked good on the chair but had withstood several years of wear, why not *knit* new upholstery fabric?

I know that it might have been easier to get an upholsterer to make new pillows for the chair, but a chair with the history of "My Chair" deserved something more personal. I located my needles and yarn and set to work. Within a short time I had made new upholstery for the chair. A little sandpaper and some furniture stain covered the cat and dog scratches and *voila*: a brand new chair.

Knitting new upholstery is a great way to spruce up a favorite old chair, especially one that has loose pillows. The pattern I used for "My Chair" is particularly good for any type of upholstery because the knit and slip stitches make a very strong fabric. You will discover that it looks just as attractive on the reverse side, and you may have trouble deciding which side of the knitted fabric to use for your upholstery.

If you must knit to a gauge, the upholstered pillows for my chair were worked at approximately 4 stitches to the inch. You can set your own gauge to get a pillow which is the approximate size given in the instructions.

SIZE: Seat: approximately 23'' x 23'' (58.5cm x 58.5cm). Back: approximately 23'' x 19'' (58.5cm x 48.5cm).

MATERIALS: Six 80-yard (73m) skeins grey Lily Rug Yarn, seven 80-yard (73m) skeins wine Lily Rug Yarn, size 6 knitting needles, foam rubber or polyester fiberfill.

PATTERN: Each row begins and ends with a knit stitch that is a selvage stitch and is not part of the pattern. The selvage will make a neater seam when assembling the upholstery. The color not in use is left at the side; do not carry it across the row.

Row 1 (grey): Knit 1. *Slip 1 as if to purl, knit 2.* Repeat from * to * across the row to the last stitch. Knit 1.
Row 2 (grey): Knit.
Row 3 (wine): Knit 1. *Knit 2, slip 1.* Repeat from * to * across the row to the last stitch. Knit 1.
Row 4 (wine): Knit.

SEAT

Top and Bottom (make 2)

DIRECTIONS: With grey, cast on 92 stitches. Knit in pattern until the piece is a square, measuring approximately 23'' x 23'' (58.5cm x 58.5cm). Bind off.

Side Strip (make 1)

DIRECTIONS: With grey, cast on 16 stitches. Knit in pattern until the piece measures 92'' (233.5cm) or until the side strip will fit around the four edges of the pillow seat.

FINISHING: Finish following the suggestions in the "Hints on Finishing" section in the appendix. Carefully block the side strip so that it will fit around the pillow. Join the short edges of the side strip. Join the long edge of the side strip to the seat top, easing to fit. Repeat for the bottom, leaving an opening for stuffing. Stuff with polyester fiberfill or a piece of foam rubber cut to size. Close the opening.

BACK

Top and Bottom (make 2)

DIRECTIONS: With grey, cast on 92 stitches. Knit in pattern until the piece measures approximately 23'' x 19'' (58.5cm x 48.5cm). Bind off.

Side Strip (make 1)

DIRECTIONS: With grey, cast on 16 stitches. Knit in pattern until the piece measures 84'' (213.5cm) or until the side strip will fit around the four edges of the pillow back.

FINISHING: Finish following the suggestions in the "Hints on Finishing" section in the appendix. Carefully block the side strip so that it will fit around the pillow. Join the short edges of the side strip. Join the long edge of the side strip to the top of the pillow back, easing to fit. Repeat for the bottom, leaving an opening for stuffing. Stuff with polyester fiberfill or a piece of foam rubber cut to size. Close the opening.

THE ROUND RUG

Round tables, round tablecloths, and especially round rugs add a warm welcome to any room. I'm sure psychologists would have something to say about why we find roundness to be so warm and appealing. (Peace treaties are usually signed at round tables, and even corporate "think tanks" display a liking for "round table" discussions.)

I'll bet you never thought of *knitting* a round rug. And why not? Once you have learned how to knit in the round, there is really nothing that you will not be able to do.

This entire rug is worked with two strands of thread. Don't be concerned if the strands get twisted as this will make an interesting effect. You begin working with a set of double-pointed needles and move onto the circular needle as soon as you have enough stitches (at about the thirteenth round). Ideally, I suppose, you should start with a small circular needle and progress to larger and larger needles, but I've found that the whole rug can be worked on a 24″ circular needle. At the end, the stitches will be crowded, and you will have to support the knitting in your lap rather than on the needle because the weight of the knitting could cause the needle to break. If you need some help with knitting in the round, see the appendix.

After the rug is completed, you may want to apply an antiskid backing to the reverse side. This can be sprayed or painted on, and will prevent slipping as well as strengthen the rug. If you have to store your rug, always roll it rather than fold it. Rug padding placed under the rug will help make the rug wear longer.

This round rug is approximately 45'' (114.5cm) in diameter, which is about the largest rug you can work comfortably on commercially made needles. If you think you'd like to try a larger circular rug, I've included a set of instructions for increasing the rug to approximately 84'' (213.5cm) in diameter. The knitting is going to be quite heavy and clumsy, however, and at the end all of it will be in your lap as you work the rounds. You're sure to impress your neighbors as well as build up the muscles in your arms.

SIZE: Approximately 45'' (114.5cm) in diameter, not including fringe.

MATERIALS: 16 ounces yellow Aunt Lydia's Heavy Rug Yarn, 13 ounces blue Aunt Lydia's Heavy Rug Yarn, size 11 double-pointed knitting needles (set of four), size 11 circular needle, tapestry needle, latex rug backing (optional).

NOTE: Always mark the start of each round by placing a safety pin in the first stitch of the round. Move this pin when you reach this stitch and replace it in the new stitch just formed.

DIRECTIONS: With two strands of blue, cast 9 stitches onto one double-pointed needle. Divide the stitches evenly onto three needles; join, being careful not to twist the stitches.
Round 1: Knit.
Round 2: Knit and purl into each stitch. (18 stitches)
Round 3: *Knit 1, purl 1.* Repeat from * to * around the round.
Round 4: *Purl 1, knit 1.* Repeat from * to * around the round.
Round 5: *Knit 1, purl 1.* Repeat from * to * around the round.
Round 6: Knit and purl into each stitch. (36 stitches)
Rounds 7, 9 and 11: *Purl 1, knit 1.* Repeat from * to * around the round.
Rounds 8, 10 and 12: *Knit 1, purl 1.* Repeat from * to * around the round.
Round 13: Knit and purl into each stitch. (72 stitches)
Rounds 14, 16, 18, 20, 22 and 24: *Purl 1, knit 1.* Repeat from * to * around the round.
Rounds 15, 17, 19, 21, 23 and 25: *Knit 1, purl 1.* Repeat from * to * around the round.
Round 26: Cut one strand of blue and attach yellow so that you are now working with one strand of blue and one of yellow. Knit and purl into each stitch. (144 stitches)
Rounds 27, 29, 31, 33, 35, 37, 39, 41, 43, 45, 47 and 49: *Purl 1, knit 1.* Repeat from * to * around the round.
Rounds 28, 30, 32, 34, 36, 38, 40, 42, 44, 46, 48 and 50: *Knit 1, purl 1.* Repeat from * to * around the round.
Round 51: Cut the blue strand and attach yellow so that you are now working with two strands of yellow. Knit and purl into each stitch. (288 stitches)
Rounds 52, 54, 56, 58, 60, 62, 64, 66, 68, 70, 72 and 74: *Purl 1, knit 1.* Repeat from * to * around the round.
Rounds 53, 55, 57, 59, 61, 63, 65, 67, 69, 71, 73 and 75: *Knit 1, purl 1.* Repeat from * to * around the round.
Round 76: Cut both yellow strands and attach two blue strands. *Purl 1, knit 1.* Repeat from * to * around the round.
Rounds 77, 79, 81, 83, 85, 87, 89 and 91: *Knit 1, purl 1.* Repeat from * to * around the round.
Rounds 78, 80, 82, 84, 86, 88 and 90: *Purl 1, knit 1.* Repeat from * to * around the round.
Bind off.

FINISHING: Finish following the suggestions in the "Hints on Finishing" section in the appendix. Following the instructions for making fringes given in the appendix, make sufficient 5 1/2'' (14cm) fringes to go around the rug. Attach as shown in the photograph. If desired, apply antiskid backing. Follow the instructions on the container.

FOR A LARGER RUG: Do not bind off after round 91. Instead, continue working with two blue strands.
Rounds 92, 94, 96 and 98: *Purl 1, knit 1.* Repeat from * to * around the round.
Rounds 93, 95, 97 and 99: *Knit 1, purl 1.* Repeat from * to * around the round.
Round 100: Cut one blue strand and attach yellow so that you are now working with one strand of blue and one of yellow. Knit and purl into each stitch. (576 stitches)
Rounds 101, 103, 105, 107, 109, 111, 113, 115, 117, 119, 121 and 123: *Purl 1, knit 1.* Repeat from * to * around the round.
Rounds 102, 104, 106, 108, 110, 112, 114, 116, 118, 120, 122 and 124: *Knit 1, purl 1.* Repeat from * to * around the round.
Round 125: Cut one blue strand and attach yellow so that you are now working with two strands of yellow. *Purl 1, knit 1.* Repeat from * to * around the round.
Rounds 126, 128, 130, 132, 134, 136, 138, 140, 142 and 144: *Knit 1, purl 1.* Repeat from * to * around the round.
Rounds 127, 129, 131, 133, 135, 137, 139, 141 and 143: *Purl 1, knit 1.* Repeat from * to * around the round.
Bind off after round 144 and finish according to the instructions for the smaller rug.

THE SCATTER RUG

One of the easiest projects for a knitter to make is a small scatter rug. Use some bulky yarn and large-sized knitting needles, cast on some stitches, work back and forth until the piece is the desired length and bind off. You have created a scatter rug!

Almost any knitting pattern can be used to make a scatter rug. In fact most of the squares used to make "Miss Marx's Afghan Done One Better" would work up into great scatter rugs. (If you have Miss Marx's Afghan in your den, why not make a scatter rug to match one of the squares?) The only stitch that you might find less

than satisfactory would be a straight stockinette stitch because it tends to curl, and you wouldn't want a scatter rug to curl. The pattern used for this particular rug is especially good because the combination of knit and slip stitches makes a fairly sturdy fabric that looks good on either side.

If you use polyester yarn, the rug will be machine washable. Spraying the rug with a soil repellent will help keep the washing problem to a minimum. If you coat the underside with an antiskid backing, or place the rug on a piece of rug padding, it will wear forever.

SIZE: Approximately 33″ x 41″ (84cm x 104cm).

MATERIALS: 13 ounces forest green Aunt Lydia's Heavy Rug Yarn, 13 ounces grass green Aunt Lydia's Heavy Rug Yarn, size 11 knitting needles, size K crochet hook (optional), latex rug backing (optional).

PATTERN: The color not in use is left at the side; do not carry it across the row.
Row 1 (forest green): Knit 2. *Slip 1 as if to purl, knit 2.* Repeat from * to * across the row. Knit 2.
Row 2 (forest green): Knit 2. Purl to the last 2 stitches. Knit 2.
Row 3 (grass green): Knit 2. *Knit 2, slip 1 as if to purl.* Repeat from * to * across the row. Knit 2.
Row 4 (grass green): Knit 2. Purl to the last 2 stitches. Knit 2.

DIRECTIONS: With forest green, cast on 88 stitches and knit 2 rows.
Work the pattern 11 times. Purl 2 rows with grass green. Repeat from * to * 3 times. Work the pattern 11 times. Knit 2 rows with forest green. Bind off.

FINISHING: Finish following the suggestions in the "Hints on Finishing" section in the appendix. Make two thick 8″ (20.5cm) tassels of grass green and two of forest green, following the instructions in the appendix. Attach at the corners. If desired, work a row of single crochet with grass green around all of the sides before attaching the tassels. If desired, apply antiskid backing. Follow the instructions on the container.

5.

THE SUN PORCH

Years ago, while we were waiting for our new home to be built, my husband and I, along with our daughters and assorted pets lived for nine months in a rented fifty-year-old farmhouse. Although many years have passed, I still cannot think fondly upon that experience. The house was cold; the plumbing creaked; the kitchen stove was a monster whose machinations I could not fathom; the windows seemed to be in the wrong places; and during the termite season, we had to fight off the winged demons as they swarmed through the cracks in the floor.

But the house did have one magnificent feature, which I incorporated into our own building plans. It had an old-fashioned sun porch—a room enclosed on three sides with huge windows and located so that its exposure took full advantage of the afternoon sun in the winter but received only the cool morning sun in the summer. Such a room needs no artificial heat because a true sun porch is only used during those hours and that time of the year when the warmth of the sun can best be utilized.

I'd really like to report that the sun porch in my own house is a true sun porch but, unfortunately, housing is too expensive today to depend upon the whims of weather. Although our sun porch is placed so that its exposure is ideal, we do have auxiliary heating to keep the room useful at all times. It's a room that makes you smile no matter how depressed you may feel. If there is any sun peeking anywhere through the clouds, the sun porch will capture it.

A sun porch is a romantic room, and sometimes when I sit there I imagine myself dressed in a beautiful white gown serving afternoon tea to lovely ladies with impeccable manners. Unfortunately, no one has time for afternoon tea anymore. Besides, my sun porch is a favorite refuge for dogs and cats who love sunning themselves, and for children who wish to rest their television-reddened eyes. My sun porch is never especially neat; after all it is a halfway-house between the outdoors and the inside.

Because our sun porch is kept heated at all times, it's a great room for plants. If you are a plant lover like I am, you'll find some great projects in this chapter. You'll also find instructions for the only kind of curtains you should use in a sun porch, curtains that will allow the sun to shine through. I have also included two projects which spend their summers outdoors and their winters on the sun porch: the patio pillows and the picnic place mat. If you use your sun porch as a family room, you may also want to consult the chapter on dens.

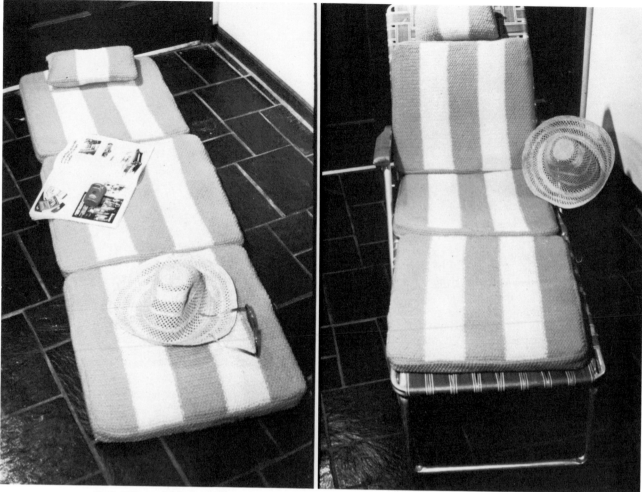

Patio Pillows as Mattress

Patio Pillows as Lounge Pad

Patio Pillows as Seats

PATIO PILLOWS

Sometimes I wonder what my family did before I made my first set of patio pillows. What did we use as a mattress for sunbathing? What did we use for a lounge pad? Where did we get those extra seats for the sun porch? A set of patio pillows can be all these things.

The patio pillows are really three large square pillows that snap together to make a mattress or a lounge pad. Individually, they can be used as extra seats for sitting on the floor. The small pillow can be used alone or as a head rest for the mattress or lounge pad.

Each pillow consists of two squares of knitting joined together with a long strip of knitting (the side strip) that fits around the four sides of the square. My pillows measure approximately 20″ x 20″ (51cm x 51cm) and were made by working to a gauge of 7 stitches = 2″ (5cm) and 15 rows = 2″ (5cm). You can use your own gauge as long as you get a pillow that is perfectly square. It really doesn't matter if the pillow is 24″ x 24″ (61cm x 61cm) or 21″ x 21″ (53.5cm x 53.5cm) provided that it is square. The side strip is approximately 2″ (5cm) wide by the necessary length.

These pillows were knitted in a moss stitch, using two colors to create a striped effect. If you prefer, however, you can knit them using almost any other stitch that you want. You may want to try one of the stitches in "Miss Marx's Afghan Done One Better."

After the pieces have been knitted, they are joined to make a square pillow. You can knit them together, crochet them together, or join them on the sewing machine, treating the pieces as you would any piece of knit fabric.

SIZE: Large pillows: approximately 20″ x 20″ (51cm x 51cm). Small pillow: approximately 7″ x 12″ (18cm x 30.5cm).

MATERIALS: 23 ounces yellow Aunt Lydia's Heavy Rug Yarn, 43 ounces orange Aunt Lydia's Heavy Rug Yarn, size 7 knitting needles, stuffing, large snap fasteners.

PATTERN: Each row begins and ends with a knit stitch that is a selvage stitch and is not part of the pattern. The selvage will make a neater seam when assembling the pillow.
Row 1: Knit 1. *Knit 1, purl 1.* Repeat from * to * across the row to the last stitch. Knit 1.
Row 2: Knit 1. *Purl 1, knit 1.* Repeat from * to * across the row to the last stitch. Knit 1.

LARGE PILLOWS
Top and Bottom (make 6)

DIRECTIONS: With orange, cast on 72 stitches.
Knit in pattern for 30 rows. Cut orange.
Attach yellow and knit in pattern for 30 rows. Cut yellow.
Attach orange and knit in pattern for 30 rows. Cut orange.
Attach yellow and knit in pattern for 30 rows. Cut yellow.
Attach orange and knit in pattern for 30 rows. Bind off with orange.

Side Strip (make 3)

DIRECTIONS: With orange, cast on 8 stitches.
Knit in pattern until piece measures 80″ (203cm), or until the side strip will fit around the four edges of the pillow.

FINISHING: Finish following the suggestions in the "Hints on Finishing" section in the appendix. Carefully block the side strips so that they will fit around the pillows. Join the short edges of one side strip. Join the long edge of the side strip to the top of one pillow, easing to fit. Repeat for the bottom, leaving an opening for stuffing. Stuff with polyester fiberfill or a piece of foam rubber cut to size. Close the opening. Repeat for the other two pillows. Sew snap fasteners to two opposite sides of the side strips of the center pillow and to one side of the side strip of the other two pillows. Make certain that the pillows are turned as they are in the photograph so that the stripe pattern will fall in the right direction when the pillows are snapped together.

SMALL PILLOW
Top and Bottom (make 2)

DIRECTIONS: With orange, cast on 26 stitches.
Knit in pattern for 30 rows. Cut orange.
Attach yellow and knit in pattern for 30 rows. Cut yellow.
Attach orange and knit in pattern for 30 rows. Bind off with orange.

FINISHING: Finish following the suggestions in the "Hints on Finishing" section in the Appendix. Join both sections of the small pillow, leaving one side open to stuff. Stuff with polyester fiberfill and close the opening.

PLANT HANGERS

I had never been very successful with house plants. Those ugly, red crockery pots in which I brought plants home from the nursery were quickly discarded and the plants transplanted to lovely planters, but with little success. For a long time I believed that instead of a green thumb I had a red hand. Then a friend who had a most successful garden of house plants told me her secret. Those crockery pots that come from the nursery are the *best* containers for your house plants. They maintain moisture and heat in the soil and do other wonderful things for the plants.

I decided, therefore, that if ugly crockery pots are necessary, they should at least be provided with beautiful coverings. What could be better than a knitted cover? Since most yarns have some elasticity, you don't have to get the cover to fit the pot exactly because the cover will mold itself to the pot—somewhat like a sweater molds itself to the body of a sweater girl. The cover is actually a little sweater for your pot. Not only will it look attractive, but it will help keep in the moisture and warmth that are necessary for growing house plants.

You may not find many nurseries sending plants home in crockery pots anymore. Most of them have resorted to those horrible plastic containers. I immediately move all of my plants into crockery pots and cover them with their sweaters.

I had been knitting covers for my plants for years and listening to the ribbing of my family and friends who found it amusing that I spent time knitting sweaters for my plants. Then books and articles started to appear, insisting not only that plants had feelings, but that you should talk to your plants and encourage them to grow. I'm ahead of the game. After all, if you were a plant with feelings, wouldn't you grow for a lady who had knitted you a sweater? Now when people ask me for my secret in growing house plants, I say, "Talk to your plants and knit them little sweaters."

If you don't really believe that knitting sweaters for your plants will help them grow, but if you like to hang plants, why not hang them in knitted plant hangers. These are extremely easy to make, and you can use scraps of yarn left over from other projects.

Here are basic instructions for four plant hangers. The small ones will hold pots approximately 4'' (10cm) in diameter or less. The medium hanger is suitable for pots approximately 5 1/2'' (14cm) in diameter, and the large hanger will hold those large hanging planters that come complete with their own plates. All of the hangers are made with heavy-duty rug yarn and size 9 double-pointed needles. Since they are all knitted in the round, you may want to refer to the appendix for hints on knitting in the round. There is almost no pot suitable for hanging that won't fit into one of these hangers because the yarn will mold itself around the pot. Use almost any combination of stitches to make these plant hangers. I've given you two patterns, but any pattern will work so long as you follow the instructions to determine the number of stitches necessary on the needles at any given time. Some additional suggestions appear in the next section on "Pot Covers."

The hangers are all made to hang from three knitted cords. If you hang a very heavy pot, you may want to reinforce the cords at the bottom and the top with some thread, or to wrap the cords around a thin wire.

If you prefer not using knitting yarn to make plant hangers, I've also given you some instructions for working with macrame cord, a more traditional material.

SMALL PLANT HANGER

MATERIALS: One ounce any heavy-duty rug yarn, size 9 double-pointed knitting needles (set of four), three stitch holders.

NOTE: Always mark the start of each round by placing a safety pin in the first stitch of the round. Move the pin when you reach this stitch and replace it in the new stitch just formed.

Basket

DIRECTIONS: Cast 9 stitches onto one double-pointed needle. Divide the stitches evenly onto three needles; join, being careful not to twist the stitches.
Round 1: Knit.
Round 2: *Knit into the front and the back of the stitch, knit 1, knit into the front and the back of the stitch.* Repeat from * to * around the round. (15 stitches)
Round 3: Knit.
Round 4: *Knit into the front and the back of the stitch, knit 3, knit into the front and the back of the stitch.* Repeat from * to * around the round. (21 stitches)
Round 5: Knit.
Round 6: *Knit into the front and the back of the stitch, knit 5, knit into the front and the back of the stitch.* Repeat from * to * around the round. (27 stitches)
Rounds 7 and 8: Knit.
Round 9: Purl across the round, placing 9 stitches on the first needle, 10 stitches on the second needle and 8 stitches on the third needle.
Round 10: Knit 1. *Yarn over, knit 2 together.* Repeat from * to * around the round.
Round 11: Knit.
Repeat rounds 10 and 11 approximately 7 times, or until the basket is the necessary size to cover the pot.

Hanging Cords

DIRECTIONS: Knit 2, bind off 7 stitches (keeping the first 2 stitches on the needle), knit 2 and place these stitches on a stitch holder, bind off 7 stitches, knit 2 stitches and place on a stitch holder, bind off 7 stitches. Knit across the first 2 stitches remaining on the needle with the second double-pointed needle.
Row 1: (Knit, winding the thread 3 times around the needle) 2 times. *Do not turn.* Slide the stitches to the other end of the double-pointed needle.
Row 2: (Knit, letting the extra wraps drop) 2 times. *Do not turn.* Slide the stitches to the other end of the double-pointed needle.
Repeat rows 1 and 2 until the cord is the desired length. (To keep the cord from curling as you work, pull on the cord before knitting the stitch.) Place the stitches on a stitch holder. Cut the yarn and attach the yarn to the second group of stitches on the stitch holder. Knit across and make the second cord in the same manner as the first. Repeat for the third cord. Place all 6 stitches on one needle and knit across all of the stitches twice. Bind off.
If desired, reinforce the cords at the bottom and top with overcast stitches.

SMALL MACRAME CORD PLANT HANGER

MATERIALS: 77 yards (2llm) three-ply jute; size 9 double-pointed knitting needles (set of four), three stitch holders.

NOTE: Always mark the start of each round by placing a safety pin in the first stitch of the round. Move the pin when you reach this stitch and replace it in the new stitch just formed.

Basket

DIRECTIONS: Cast 9 stitches onto one double-pointed needle. Divide the stitches evenly onto three needles; join, being careful not to twist the stitches.
Round 1: Knit.
Round 2: *Knit into the front and the back of the stitch, knit 1, knit into the front and the back of the stitch.* Repeat from * to * around the round. (15 stitches)
Round 3: Knit.
Round 4: *Knit into the front and the back of the stitch, knit 3, knit into the front and the back of the stitch.* Repeat from * to * around the round. (21 stitches)
Round 5: Knit.
Round 6: *Knit into the front and the back of the stitch, knit 5, knit into the front and the back of the stitch.* Repeat from * to * around the round. (27 stitches)
Rounds 7 and 8: Knit.
Round 9: Purl across the round, placing 9 stitches on the first needle, 10 stitches on the second needle and 8 stitches on the third needle.
Round 10: Knit 1. *Yarn over, knit 2 together.* Repeat from * to * around the round.
Round 11: Knit.
Repeat rounds 10 and 11 until the basket reaches the rim of the pot.

Rim

Round 1: Knit into the front and the back of the stitch, knit 7, (knit into the front and the back of the stitch) 2 times, knit 8, (knit into the front and the back of the stitch) 2 times, knit 6, knit into the front and the back of the stitch. (33 stitches)

Round 2: Knit 1. *Yarn over, knit 2 together.* Repeat from * to * around the round.

Round 3: Knit.

Round 4: Knit 1. *Yarn over, knit 2 together.* Repeat from * to * around the round.

Round 5: Knit into the front and the back of the stitch, knit 9, (knit into the front and the back of the stitch) 2 times, knit 10, (knit into the front and the back of the stitch) 2 times, knit 8, knit into the front and the back of the stitch. (39 stitches)

Round 6: Knit 1. *Yarn over, knit 2 together.* Repeat from * to * around the round.

Round 7: Knit into the front and the back of the stitch, knit 11, (knit into the front and the back of the stitch) 2 times, knit 12, (knit into the front and the back of the stitch) 2 times, knit 10, knit into the front and the back of the stitch. (45 stitches)

Hanging Cords

DIRECTIONS: Knit 2, bind off 13 stitches (keeping the first 2 stitches on the needle), knit 2 and place these stitches on a stitch holder, bind off 13 stitches, knit 2 stitches and place on a stitch holder, bind off 13 stitches. Knit across the first 2 stitches remaining on the needle with the second double-pointed needle.

Row 1: (Knit, winding the thread 3 times around the needle) 2 times. *Do not turn.* Slide the stitches to the other end of the double-pointed needle.

Row 2: (Knit, letting the extra wraps drop) 2 times. *Do not turn.* Slide the stitches to the other end of the double-pointed needle.

Repeat rows 1 and 2 until the cord is the desired length. (To keep the cord from curling as you work, pull on the cord before knitting the stitch.) Place the stitches on a stitch holder. Cut the yarn and attach the yarn to the second group of stitches on the stitch holder. Knit across and make the second cord in the same manner as the first. Repeat for the third cord. Place all 6 stitches on one needle and knit across all of the stitches twice. Bind off.

If desired, reinforce the cords at the bottom and top with overcast stitches.

MEDIUM PLANT HANGER

MATERIALS: One ounce any heavy-duty rug yarn, size 9 double-pointed knitting needles (set of four), three stitch holders.

NOTE: Always mark the start of each round by placing a safety pin in the first stitch of the round. Move the pin when you reach this stitch and replace it in the new stitch just formed.

Basket

DIRECTIONS: Cast 9 stitches onto one double-pointed needle. Divide the stitches evenly onto three needles; join, being careful not to twist the stitches.

Round 1: Knit.

Round 2: *Knit into the front and the back of the stitch, knit 1, knit into the front and the back of the stitch.* Repeat from * to * around the round. (15 stitches)

Round 3: Knit.

Round 4: *Knit into the front and the back of the stitch, knit 3, knit into the front and the back of the stitch.* Repeat from * to * around the round. (21 stitches)

Round 5: Knit.

Round 6: *Knit into the front and the back of the stitch, knit 5, knit into the front and the back of the stitch.* Repeat from * to * around the round. (27 stitches)

Round 7: Knit.

Round 8: *Knit into the front and the back of the stitch, knit 7, knit into the front and the back of the stitch.* Repeat from * to * around the round. (33 stitches)

Round 9: Knit.

Round 10: *Knit into the front and the back of the stitch, knit 9, knit into the front and the back of the stitch.* Repeat from * to * around the round. (39 stitches)

Round 11: Knit.

Round 12: Purl around the round, placing 13 stitches on the first needle, 14 stitches on the second needle and 12 stitches on the third needle.

Round 13: Knit 1. *Yarn over, knit 2 together.* Repeat from * to * around the round.

Round 14: Knit.

Repeat rounds 13 and 14 until the basket is the necessary size to cover the pot.

Hanging Cords

DIRECTIONS: Knit 2, bind off 11 stitches (keeping the first 2 stitches on the needle), knit 2 and place these stitches on a stitch holder, bind off 11 stitches, knit 2 stitches and place on a stitch holder, bind off 11 stitches. Knit across the first 2 stitches remaining on the needle with the second double-pointed needle.

Row 1: (Knit, winding the thread 3 times around the needle) 2 times. *Do not turn.* Slide the stitches to the other end of the double-pointed needle.

Row 2: (Knit, letting the extra wraps drop) 2 times. *Do not turn.* Slide the stitches to the other end of the double-pointed needle.

Repeat rows 1 and 2 until the cord is the desired length. (To keep the cord from curling as you work, pull on the cord before knitting the stitch.) Place the stitches on a stitch holder. Cut the yarn and attach the yarn to the second group of stitches on the stitch holder. Knit across and make the second cord in the same manner as the first. Repeat for the third cord. Place all 6 stitches on one needle and knit across all of the stitches twice. Bind off.

If desired, reinforce the cords at the bottom and top with overcast stitches.

LARGE PLANT HANGER

MATERIALS: 1 1/2 ounces any heavy-duty rug yarn, size 9 double-pointed knitting needles (set of four), three stitch holders.

NOTE: Always mark the start of each round by placing a safety pin in the first stitch of the round. Move the pin when you reach this stitch and replace it in the new stitch just formed.

Basket

DIRECTIONS: Cast 9 stitches onto one double-pointed needle. Divide the stitches evenly onto three needles; join, being careful not to twist the stitches.
Round 1: Knit.
Round 2: *Knit into the front and the back of the stitch, knit 1, knit into the front and the back of the stitch.* Repeat from * to * around the round. (15 stitches)
Round 3: Knit.
Round 4: *Knit into the front and the back of the stitch, knit 3, knit into the front and the back of the stitch.* Repeat from * to * around the round. (21 stitches)
Round 5: Knit.
Round 6: *Knit into the front and the back of the stitch, knit 5, knit into the front and the back of the stitch.* Repeat from * to * around the round. (27 stitches)
Round 7: Knit.
Round 8: *Knit into the front and the back of the stitch, knit 7, knit into the front and the back of the stitch.* Repeat from * to * around the round. (33 stitches)
Round 9: Knit.
Round 10: *Knit into the front and the back of the stitch, knit 9, knit into the front and the back of the stitch.* Repeat from * to * around the round. (39 stitches)
Round 11: Knit.
Round 12: Purl around the round, placing 13 stitches on the first needle, 14 stitches on the second needle and 12 stitches on the third needle.
Round 13: *Knit, winding the thread 3 times around the needle.* Repeat from * to * around the round.

Round 14: *Knit, allowing the extra wraps to drop.* Repeat from * to * around the round.
Repeat rounds 13 and 14 until the basket is the necessary size to cover the pot. (*Note: The stitch used here is extremely resilient and will expand to fit a large pot.*)

Edging and Hanging Cords

DIRECTIONS: Knit 2 and put the stitches on a stitch holder. Knit 1, (knit 2 together, yarn over, knit 2 together; turn, purl 1, work 5 stitches in the yarn over—*to work 5 stitches in 1 stitch (knit 1, purl 1) 2 times, knit 1 in the same stitch*—purl 1, slip 1; turn, bind off 7 stitches—1 stitch will remain on the right-hand needle) 3 times. Knit 1 and place the 2 stitches on a stitch holder. Knit 1, (knit 2 together, yarn over, knit 2 together; turn, purl 1, work 5 stitches in the yarn over, purl 1, slip 1; turn, bind off 7 stitches—1 stitch will remain on the right-hand needle) 3 times. Knit 1 and place these 2 stitches on a stitch holder. Knit 1, (knit 2 together, yarn over, knit 2 together; turn, purl 1, work 5 stitches in the yarn over, purl 1, slip 1; turn, bind off 7 stitches—1 stitch will remain on the right-hand needle) 3 times. Bind off the remaining stitch. Knit across the 2 stitches on the first stitch holder.
Row 1: (Knit, winding the thread 3 times around the needle) 2 times. *Do not turn.* Slide the stitches to the other end of the double-pointed needle.
Row 2: (Knit, letting the extra wraps drop) 2 times. *Do not turn.* Slide the stitches to the other end of the double-pointed needle.
Repeat rows 1 and 2 until the cord is the desired length. (To keep the cord from curling as you work, pull on the cord before knitting the stitch.) Place the stitches on a stitch holder. Cut the yarn and attach the yarn to the second group of stitches on the stitch holder. Knit across and make the second cord in the same manner as the first. Repeat for the third cord. Place all 6 stitches on one needle and knit across all of the stitches twice. Bind off.
If desired, reinforce the cords at the bottom and top with overcast stitches.

POT COVERS

If you don't like to hang plants, you can knit attractive covers for them. The covers will allow you the luxury of keeping your pots planted in their ugly but utilitarian pots. Covers can be knitted in any color to match your decor. You may want to remove the pot from its cover when you water the plant, but the cover will slip back on easily. In case a little moisture seeps through, your knitted pot covers will soak it up without a complaint.

Here are instructions for three different pot covers. Each of them will fit a pot of almost any size because the cover will mold itself to the pot. Any of them can be used as a plant hanger simply by attaching cords. The striped cover is a good project for using up extra bits of yarn left over from other projects. It can be done in two colors, as in the sample, or in any number of colors you wish. Search around the house for odd bits of yarn. (I find the backs of unused dresser drawers a great spot for scavenging for leftover yarn that I meant to return to the knitting shop at least five years ago—before the shop went out of business.) The woven basket makes up into a pot cover that looks like a straw basket. In fact, it makes a nice vase for holding dried flowers.

POT COVER WITH SCALLOPED EDGING

MATERIALS: One ounce any heavy-duty rug yarn, small amount of heavy-duty rug yarn in contrasting color, size 9 double-pointed needles (set of four).

NOTE: Always mark the start of each round by placing a safety pin in the first stitch of the round. Move the pin when you reach this stitch and replace it in the new stitch just formed.

Basket

DIRECTIONS: Cast 9 stitches onto one double-pointed needle. Divide the stitches evenly onto three needles; join, being careful not to twist the stitches.
Round 1: Knit.
Round 2: *Knit into the front and the back of the stitch, knit 1, knit into the front and the back of the stitch.* Repeat from * to * around the round. (15 stitches)
Round 3: Knit.

Round 4: *Knit into the front and the back of the stitch, knit 3, knit into the front and the back of the stitch.* Repeat from * to * around the round.
Round 5: Knit.
Round 6: *Knit into the front and the back of the stitch, knit 5, knit into the front and the back of the stitch.* Repeat from * to * around the round. (27 stitches)
Round 7: Knit.
Round 8: *Knit into the front and the back of the stitch, knit 7, knit into the front and the back of the stitch.* Repeat from * to * around the round. (33 stitches)
Round 9: Knit.
Round 10: *Knit into the front and the back of the stitch, knit 9, knit into the front and the back of the stitch.* Repeat from * to * around the round. (39 stitches)
Round 11: Knit.
Round 12: Purl around the round, placing 13 stitches on the first needle, 14 stitches on the second needle and 12 stitches on the third needle.
Round 13: Knit 1. *Yarn over, knit 2 together.* Repeat from * to * around the round.
Round 14: Knit.
Repeat rounds 13 and 14 until the pot cover is the necessary size to cover the pot.

Edging

DIRECTIONS: Cut the main color and attach the contrasting color. Knit 1. *Knit 2 together, yarn over, knit 2 together; turn, purl 1, work 5 stitches in the yarn over— *to work 5 stitches in 1 stitch (knit 1, purl 1) 2 times, knit 1 in the same stitch*—purl 1, slip 1; turn, bind off 7 stitches (1 stitch will remain on the right-hand needle).* Repeat from * to * around the round to the last 2 stitches. Knit 1, yarn over, knit 1; turn, purl 1, work 5 stitches in the yarn over, purl 1, slip 1; turn, bind off the remaining stitches.

STRIPED POT COVER

MATERIALS: One ounce any heavy-duty rug yarn (at least two colors), size 9 double-pointed needles (set of four).

NOTE: Always mark the start of each round by placing a safety pin in the first stitch of each round. Move the pin when you reach this stitch and replace it in the new stitch just formed.

Basket

DIRECTIONS: With the first color, cast 9 stitches onto one double-pointed needle. Divide the stitches evenly onto three needles; join, being careful not to twist the stitches.
Round 1: Knit.
Round 2: *Knit into the front and the back of the stitch, knit 1, knit into the front and the back of the stitch.* Repeat from * to * around the round. (15 stitches)
Round 3: Knit.
Round 4: *Knit into the front and the back of the stitch, knit 3, knit into the front and the back of the stitch.* Repeat from * to * around the round. (21 stitches)
Round 5: Knit.
Round 6: *Knit into the front and the back of the stitch, knit 5, knit into the front and the back of the stitch.* Repeat from * to * around the round. (27 stitches)
Round 7: Knit.
Round 8: *Knit into the front and the back of the stitch, knit 7, knit into the front and the back of the stitch.* Repeat from * to * around the round. (33 stitches)
Round 9: Knit.
Round 10: *Knit into the front and the back of the stitch, knit 9, knit into the front and the back of the stitch.* Repeat from * to * around the round. (39 stitches)
Round 11: Knit.
Rounds 12, 13 and 14: Purl.
Round 15: Cut first color; attach second color. Knit.
Rounds 16 and 17: Knit.
Round 18: Cut second color; attach first color. Purl.
Rounds 19 and 20: Purl.
Repeat rows 15, 16, 17, 18, 19 and 20 until the pot cover is the desired height, ending with row 20.

Edging

DIRECTIONS: Cut first color; attach second color. Knit 1. *Knit 2 together, yarn over, knit 2 together; turn, purl 1, work 5 stitches in the yarn over—*to work 5 stitches in 1 stitch (knit 1, purl 1) 2 times, knit 1 in the same stitch*—purl 1, slip 1; turn, bind off 7 stitches (1 stitch will remain on the right-hand needle).* Repeat from * to * around the round to the last 2 stitches. Knit 1, yarn over, knit 1; turn, purl 1, work 5 stitches in the yarn over, purl 1, slip 1; turn, bind off the remaining stitches.

WOVEN BASKET POT COVER

MATERIAL: One ounce any heavy-duty rug yarn, size 9 double-pointed needles (set of four).

NOTE: Always mark the start of each round by placing a safety pin in the first stitch of the round. Move the pin when you reach this stitch and replace it in the new stitch just formed.

DIRECTIONS: Cast 9 stitches onto one double-pointed needle. Divide the stitches evenly onto three needles; join, being careful not to twist the stitches.
Round 1: Knit.
Round 2: *Knit and purl into the stitch, knit 1, knit and purl into the stitch.* Repeat from * to * around the round. (15 stitches)
Round 3: *Knit 1, slip 2 as if to purl.* Repeat from * to * around the round.
Round 4: (Knit and purl into the stitch, knit 2) 4 times, knit and purl into the stitch, knit 1, knit and purl into the stitch. (21 stitches)
Round 5: *Knit 1, slip 2.* Repeat from * to * around the round.
Round 6: Purl 1, knit 2. *Knit and purl into the stitch, knit 2.* Repeat from * to * around the round. (27 stitches)
Round 7: *Knit 1, slip 2.* Repeat from * to * around the round.
Round 8: *(Knit and purl into the stitch, knit 2) 2 times, purl 1, knit 2.* Repeat from * to * around the round. (33 stitches)
Round 9: *Knit 1, slip 2.* Repeat from * to * around the round.
Round 10: *(Knit and purl into the stitch, knit 2) 2 times, purl 1, knit 2, purl 1, knit 1.* Repeat from * to * around the round. (39 stitches)
Round 11: *Knit 1, slip 2.* Repeat from * to * around the round.
Round 12: Purl 1, knit 2. *(Knit and purl into the stitch, knit 2) 2 times, (purl 1, knit 2) 2 times.* Repeat from * to * around the round. (45 stitches)
Round 13: *Knit 1, slip 2.* Repeat from * to * around the round.
Round 14: *Purl 1, knit 2.* Repeat from * to * around the round. Repeat rounds 13 and 14 until the pot cover is the desired height. Purl 2 rows and bind off loosely.

AFRICAN VIOLET POT COVER

If you want to cover a pot of African violets or one containing some beautiful forced daffodils or narcissus, you certainly don't want a pot cover that looks like a sweater. For something as delicate as African violets, an attractive cover would be one that looks like a piece of old-fashioned lace. Here is a special pot cover for those delicate house plants in your collection.

Instead of heavy-duty rug yarn, use a fine crochet cotton, but work with large needles. This will make the work go fast and will produce a lacy piece of knitting. Actually, you will knit a very large, round doily. Rounds 1 to 15 will become the bottom of the pot cover and the rest of the doily will become the sides. For hints on knitting in the round, see the appendix.

When the knitting has been completed it must be stiffened, using the old sugar-water method, and then molded to the pot that will receive your plant. If you want to keep a plate under your pot, just mold the sugar-stiffened doily around the pot as it sits on the plate. When the knitting has dried, you can place your plant into the pot. It's not a good idea to try to dry the knitting over a pot that has already been planted because in drying out the knitting, you may reduce the moisture needed by the plant.

MATERIALS: One 218-yard (200m) ball DMC Brilliant Crochet Cotton, size 9 double-pointed knitting needles (set of four), size 9 circular knitting needle, crockery planter, sugar, water.

NOTE: Always mark the start of each round by placing a safety pin in the first stitch of the round. Move the pin when you reach this stitch and replace it in the new stitch just formed.

Basket

DIRECTIONS: Cast 9 stitches onto one double-pointed needle. Divide the stitches evenly onto three needles; join, being careful not to twist the stitches.
Round 1: Knit.
Round 2: *Knit into the front and the back of the stitch, knit 1, knit into the front and the back of the stitch.* Repeat from * to * around the round. (15 stitches)
Round 3: Knit.
Round 4: *Knit into the front and the back of the stitch, knit 3, knit into the front and the back of the stitch.* Repeat from * to * around the round. (21 stitches)
Round 5: Knit.
Round 6: *Knit into the front and the back of the stitch, knit 5, knit into the front and the back of the stitch.* Repeat from * to * around the round. (27 stitches)
Round 7: Knit.
Round 8: *Knit into the front and the back of the stitch, knit 7, knit into the front and the back of the stitch.* Repeat from * to * around the round. (33 stitches)
Round 9: Knit.

Round 10: *Knit into the front and the back of the stitch, knit 9, knit into the front and the back of the stitch.* Repeat from * to * around the round. (39 stitches)
Round 11: Knit.
Round 12: *Knit into the front and the back of the stitch, knit 11, knit into the front and the back of the stitch.* Repeat from * to * around the round. (45 stitches)
Round 13: Knit.
Round 14: *Knit into the front and the back of the stitch, knit 13, knit into the front and the back of the stitch.* Repeat from * to * around the round. (51 stitches)
Round 15: Knit.
Round 16: *Yarn over, knit 1.* Repeat from * to * around the round. (102 stitches)
Rounds 17, 18 and 19: Knit.
Round 20: *Yarn over, knit 2 together.* Repeat from * to * around the round to the last 3 stitches. (Yarn over, knit 1) 3 times. (105 stitches)
Rounds 21, 22 and 23: Knit.
Repeat rounds 20, 21, 22 and 23 until the piece is the desired height of the pot cover, measuring from round 16.

Edging

DIRECTIONS: Knit 1. *Knit 2 together, yarn over, knit 2 together; turn, purl 1, work 9 stitches in the yarn over—*to work 9 stitches in 1 stitch (knit 1, purl 1) 4 times, knit 1 in the same stitch—*purl 1, slip 1; turn, bind off 11 stitches (1 stitch will remain on the right-hand needle).* Repeat from * to * around the round to the last stitch. Bind off the last stitches.

FINISHING: Mix 1/3 cup of sugar with 4 tablespoons of water until the sugar has started to dissolve. Heat the solution on the stove until the sugar is completely dissolved. Remove the solution from the heat and soak the knitting in the solution until it is completely wet and most of the sugar water has been absorbed. Let cool slightly. Wring out the knitting and shape it over the inverted pot. Place the pot and the knitting in a warm place to dry. This may take several days. When the knitting is completely dry and no longer sticky, the plant may be planted in the pot.

LACE CURTAINS

Her neighbors knew that my mother-in-law was involved in a perpetual love affair with curtains. For her, no house was complete—no matter how elegant the furniture or carpeting—unless every window was properly curtained or draped. I have gone with her to visit the new homes of relatives, and while they were pointing out the wonderful features of the new house, she was mentally measuring the windows so that within a few days she could present her unique housewarming gift, a finished set of curtains. She had the uncanny ability of knowing exactly how long and how wide to make a set of curtains without ever making use of a yardstick.

For her, every room in the house needed its own particular curtains. I remember once hanging café curtains in the living room; I thought it a real decorating coup. She excused my mistake with a question, "Why did you put the kitchen curtains in here?" As usual, she was right. For my mother-in-law, a curtain served not only to provide privacy but also to set the tone for a room. A formal room might need a set of formal drapes, which could be drawn across the window not only to shut out the sun or the view of a prying neighbor, but also to add a bright note of color to a drab wall. A child's room needed curtains to make a child laugh, so they were made from fabric studded with balloons and jumping clowns. Kitchen curtains needed color and charm because so much time was spent in the kitchen. She loved shopping for fabrics, and it was always a delight to see her face light up when she found just the right combination for a particular room even though she might not yet have seen the room. She knew that someday this fabric would make "wonderful kitchen curtains" for someone's house. The results of her individuality and good taste still hang on many windows despite her death a number of years ago.

Although we now live in a house set off by woods, where curtains are not needed for privacy, my mother-in-law's training has convinced me that some kind of curtain treatment is necessary for every room. Big gaping windows without curtains might look fine during the day when they frame a beautiful view, but at night, as she would say, "You have those big black holes looking at you."

The sun porch windows presented a tricky problem—how to devise a curtain that would not cut sunlight but would provide enough coverage to hide those "big black holes." Had my mother-in-law lived to help decorate the sun porch, I know she would have had a solution immediately. It took me a little while longer, but I have felt over the years that my solution would have pleased her. The curtains I eventually hung in my sun porch fulfill her criteria for good curtains: they are unique, utilitarian, and decorative. My sun porch curtains are knitted lace!

This is one project for which some understanding of gauge may be necessary because you will want to make

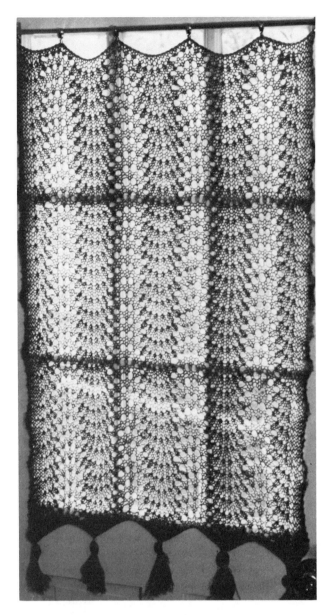

your curtains cover a predetermined width. In my curtains each pattern repeat equals approximately 5″ (12.5cm). To make the curtain wider, cast on an extra 17 stitches for every additional pattern repeat needed. In order to keep the patterns even, you will only be able to increase or decrease in multiples of 5″ (12.5cm), or whatever gauge your knitting of the 17 stitches in the pattern will produce. Remember that it is always better to make the curtain wider since it will hang better when it is fuller. My mother-in-law's rule of thumb was always to make a curtain four times the width of the window; otherwise she felt the curtain would look skimpy.

My curtains were made using two strands of crochet cotton, but you can make these curtains with other types of thread, such as butcher twine or macrame cord, as well.

SIZE: 22″ x 44″ (56cm x 112cm). (See above for instructions on changing dimensions.)

MATERIALS: Eight 100-yard (91.5m) balls Coats & Clark Speed-Cro-Sheen or Lily Mills Double Quick, size 11 knitting needles, café curtain rings, tapestry needle.

DIRECTIONS: With two strands, cast on 78 stitches. (*Note: Entire curtain is worked with two strands of thread.*)

Rows 1, 2, 3, 4, 5 and 6: Knit.

Row 7: Knit 5. *(Purl 2 together) 3 times, (yarn over, knit 1) 5 times, yarn over, (purl 2 together) 3 times.* Repeat from * to * across the row to the last 5 stitches. Knit 5.

Row 8: Knit 5, purl 68, knit 5.

Row 9: Knit.

Row 10: Knit 5, purl 68, knit 5.

Repeat rows 7, 8, 9, and 10 until the curtain is the desired length, ending with row 7. Bind off loosely.

FINISHING: Finish following the special suggestions for finishing lace projects in the "Hints on Finishing" section in the appendix. Block to the desired length and width. To give the curtain more body, add more starch. Make five 5″ (13cm) tassels according to the instructions in the appendix, and attach with a tapestry needle to each point along the bottom. Attach rings to each point along the top and hang.

PICNIC PLACE MAT

A loaf of bread, a jug of wine, a book of verse, and it's a picnic anytime of the year! My family loves picnics.

For these occasions I've made a special set of picnic place mats. They are rustic enough to convey the feeling of eating outdoors, strong enough to withstand the sloppy kind of eating that accompanies picnic feasts, and will wipe clean quite easily.

The place mats are made with macrame cord. I won't fool you by telling you that macrame cord is easy to knit with. Unlike cotton, wool, or synthetics, it has very little elasticity. After a few rows it starts to dig into your fingers, but the place mats are easy to make, and you can probably make a whole set in an afternoon or two.

Basically each place mat is a large, round doily that is begun on four double-pointed needles and then switched at about the twelfth row to a circular needle or continued on the four needles. For special hints on knitting in the round, see the appendix.

SIZE: Approximately 13″ (33cm) in diameter.

MATERIALS: 77 yards (211m) three-ply jute (for each set of two), size 11 double-pointed knitting needles (set of four), size 11 circular needle.

NOTE: Always mark the start of each round by placing a safety pin in the first stitch of the round. Move the pin when you reach this stitch and replace it in the new stitch just formed.

DIRECTIONS: Cast 9 stitches onto one double-pointed needle. Divide the stitches onto three needles; join, being careful not to twist the stitches.

Round 1: Knit.

Round 2: *Yarn over, knit 1.* Repeat from * to * around the round. (18 stitches)

Rounds 3, 4 and 5: Knit.

Round 6: *Yarn over, knit 1.* Repeat from * to * around the round. (36 stitches)

Rounds 7, 8, 9, 10, 11 and 12: Knit.

Round 13: *Yarn over, knit 1, yarn over, knit 3.* Repeat from * to * around the round to the last 3 stitches. Yarn over, knit 1, yarn over, knit 2. (54 stitches)

Rounds 14, 15 and 16: Knit.

Round 17: Knit 1. *(Yarn over, knit 1) 3 times, yarn over, knit 3.* Repeat from * to * around the round to the last 5 stitches. (Yarn over, knit 1) 3 times, yarn over, knit 2. (90 stitches)

Rounds 18, 19 and 20: Knit.
Bind off loosely.

FINISHING: Shape by pressing with a warm steam iron over a damp cloth.

6.

THE BATHROOM

To the teen-agers in my household, the bathroom is the most important room in the house. If the living room or dining room were devoured by an earthquake, they would survive. Even destruction of the kitchen would not distress them; they could make do with pretzels and trips to a pizza parlor. But if a "closed for repairs" sign appeared on our bathroom doors, there would be instant mutiny among the troops.

Besides its intended use as a place for personal hygiene, in our house the bathroom is alternately a library, a beauty salon, a makeup parlor, a dental clinic, and a barber shop for teen-agers. Give a teen-ager a good book or the latest charm magazine, and she will disappear into the bathroom for hours, or until someone starts pounding on the door. Every new hair style has to be practiced in front of the bathroom mirror to the accompaniment of a whir from the blow dryer, which automatically disturbs every other electrical appliance in the house.

New makeup, most of it never worn again, must be applied and tested in the bathroom. Eyes are made bigger and smaller, farther apart or closer together according to the instructions in the latest charm magazine. Cheeks are made red, brown or purple depending upon what colors are promoted that year. Gobs of cream and skin preparations are alternately put on and taken off of faces. And all of this must take place in front of the bathroom mirror despite the fact that the house boasts mirrors in almost every room.

Teeth are not just brushed; they are water-picked and polished. Even baths are not simple washes; they are beauty rituals with bubbles, bath salts and perfumes befitting a Roman potentate. Hair is never cut in a barber shop or a beauty shop. "He'll take too much off." Ends are always trimmed in—you guessed it—the bathroom.

Since my family spends so much time in the bathroom, decorating the room became extremely important. No one has ever questioned the knitted pieces in the bathroom because the bathroom is the one room where knitted articles are probably more practical than anything else. They are warm, and they are able to withstand steam as well as to absorb moisture.

In this chapter, you will find a complete knitted bathroom ensemble: bathroom rug, toilet seat cover, tank lid cover, tissue box cover and toilet tissue cover. The pattern used for the entire ensemble is a variation of the two-color ladder stitch that appears in "Miss Marx's Afghan Done One Better." This combination of knit and slip stitches makes a very sturdy fabric. For you traditionalists, the gauge used in the photographed models was 4 stitches = 1'' (2.5cm) and 6 rows = 1'' (2.5cm).

BATHROOM RUG

SIZE: Approximately 34″ x 30″ (86.5cm x 76cm).

MATERIALS: Four 80-yard (73m) skeins brown Lily Rug Yarn, four 80-yard (73m) skeins orange Lily Rug Yarn, four 80-yard (73m) skeins yellow Lily Rug Yarn, size 9 knitting needles, latex rug backing (optional).

RIBBING PATTERN: The color not in use is left at the side and not carried across the row. Work with either three balls or three bobbins of the three colors used for the ribbing pattern. *To avoid holes when joining colors, always bring the new color from underneath.*

Row 1: Brown: (Knit 2, purl 2) 10 times, knit 2.
   Yellow: (Purl 2, knit 2) 10 times, purl 2.
   Orange: (Knit 2, purl 2) 10 times, purl 1.
Row 2: Orange: Knit 1 (knit 2, purl 2) 10 times.
   Yellow: (Knit 2, purl 2) 10 times, knit 2.
   Brown: (Purl 2, knit 2) 10 times, purl 2.

BODY PATTERN: The color not in use is left at the side; do not carry it across the row. Work with three balls or three bobbins of the colors used. *To avoid holes when joining colors, always bring the new color from underneath.*

Row 1: Brown: Knit 2, slip 1 as if to purl, (knit 5, slip 1 as if to purl) 6 times, knit 3.

Yellow: Knit 2, slip 1 as if to purl, (knit 5, slip 1 as if to purl) 6 times, knit 3.
Orange: Knit 2, slip 1 as if to purl, (knit 5, slip 1 as if to purl) 6 times, knit 2.
Row 2: Purl all of the knit stitches and slip all of the slip stitches, using the same colors as row 1.
Row 3: Yellow: (Knit 5, slip 1 as if to purl) 7 times.
   Orange: (Knit 5, slip 1 as if to purl) 7 times.
   Brown: (Knit 5, slip 1 as if to purl) 6 times, knit 5.
Row 4: Using the same colors as row 3: *Knit 5, wool forward, slip 1 as if to purl, wool back.* Repeat from * to * to the last 5 stitches. Knit 5.

DIRECTIONS: With brown, cast on 125 stitches. Work in the ribbing pattern (attaching the yellow and orange where necessary) until the piece measures approximately 2 1/2″ (6.5cm).
Work in body pattern until the piece is approximately 31 1/2″ (80cm) long.
Work in ribbing pattern until piece is approximately 34″ (86.5cm) long or the desired length.
Bind off with brown.

FINISHING: Finish following the suggestions in the "Hints on Finishing" section in the appendix. If desired, apply antiskid backing. Follow the instructions on the container.

TOILET TANK LID COVER

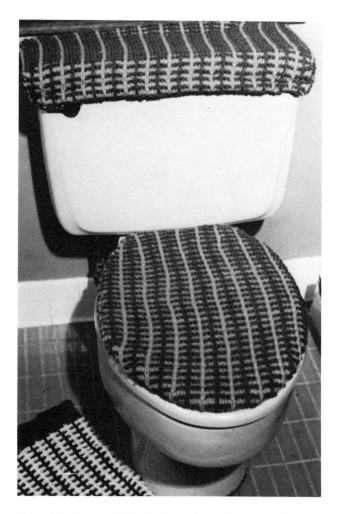

SIZE: Standard tank lid.

MATERIALS: Three 80-yard (73m) skeins brown Lily Rug Yarn, three 80-yard (73m) skeins orange Lily Rug Yarn, size 9 knitting needles, large-eyed tapestry needle, 1 yard (.9m) 1/2" (13mm) elastic.

DIRECTIONS: With brown, cast on 83 stitches. Attach orange. The color not in use is left at the side; do not carry it across the row.

Row 1 (orange): Knit 2, slip 1 as if to purl, (knit 5, slip 1 as if to purl) 13 times, knit 2.

Row 2 (orange): Purl all of the knit stitches and slip all of the slip stitches.

Row 3 (brown): (Knit 5, slip 1 as if to purl) 13 times, knit 5.

Row 4 (brown): (Knit 5, wool forward, slip 1 as if to purl, wool back) 13 times, knit 5.

Rows 5, 9, 13 and 17 (orange): Repeat row 1.

Rows 6, 10, 14 and 18 (orange): Repeat row 2.

Rows 7, 11, 15 and 19 (brown): Repeat row 3.

Rows 8, 12, 16 and 20 (brown): Repeat row 4.

Row 21 (orange): Knit 2, slip 1 as if to purl, (knit 5, slip 1 as if to purl) 13 times, knit 2.

Row 22 (orange): Purl all of the knit stitches of the previous row and slip all of the slip stitches. Cut orange thread.

Row 23 (brown): Cast on 12 stitches at the beginning of the row, and work across the entire row in this manner: (knit 5, slip 1 as if to purl) 15 times, knit 5. (95 stitches)

Row 24 (brown): Cast on 12 stitches at the beginning of the row and work across the entire row in this manner: (Knit 5, wool forward, slip 1 as if to purl, wool back) 17 times, knit 5. Attach orange thread. (107 stitches)

Row 25 (orange): Knit 2, slip 1 as if to purl, (knit 5, slip 1) 17 times, knit 2.

Row 26 (orange): Purl all of the knit stitches of the previous row and slip all of the slip stitches.

Row 27 (brown): (Knit 5, slip 1 as if to purl) 17 times, knit 5.

Row 28 (brown): (Knit 5, wool forward, slip 1 as if to purl, wool back) 17 times, knit 5.

Rows 29–76: Repeat rows 25, 26, 27 and 28.

Row 77 (orange): Knit 2, slip 1 as if to purl, (knit 5, slip 1 as if to purl) 17 times, knit 2.

Row 78 (orange): Purl all of the knit stitches of the previous row and slip all of the slip stitches. Cut orange thread.

Row 79 (brown): Bind off the first 12 stitches. (Knit 5, slip 1 as if to purl) 15 times, knit 5. (95 stitches)

Row 80 (brown): Bind off the first 12 stitches. (Knit 5, wool forward, slip 1 as if to purl, wool back) 13 times, knit 5. Attach orange thread. (83 stitches)

Row 81 (orange): Knit 2, slip 1 as if to purl, (knit 5, slip 1 as if to purl) 13 times, knit 2.

Row 82 (orange): Purl all of the knit stitches of the previous row and slip all of the slip stitches.

Row 83 (brown): (Knit 5, slip 1) 13 times, knit 5.

Row 84 (brown): (Knit 5, wool forward, slip 1 as if to purl, wool back) 13 times, knit 5.

Rows 85–96: Repeat rows 81, 82, 83 and 84.

Row 97 (orange): Knit 2, slip 1 as if to purl, (knit 5, slip 1 as if to purl) 13 times, knit 2.

Row 98 (orange): Purl all of the knit stitches of the previous row and slip all of the slip stitches.

Row 99 (brown): (Knit 5, slip 1 as if to purl) 13 times, knit 5.

Bind off with brown.

FINISHING: Finish following the suggestions in the "Hints on Finishing" section in the appendix. Sew the edges together along the four corners. Make a casing by making a 1" (2.5cm) hem along the inside of the cover, leaving an opening for threading the elastic. Cut the elastic to the exact measurement of the tank lid, thread it through the casing and stitch the ends together.

TOILET SEAT COVER

SIZE: Standard toilet seat lid.

MATERIALS: Two 80-yard (73m) skeins brown Lily Rug Yarn, two 80-yard (73m) skeins orange Lily Rug Yarn, size 9 knitting needles.

Seat Cover Top

DIRECTIONS: With brown cast on 17 stitches. Attach orange. The color not in use is left at the side; do not carry it across the row.

Row 1 (orange): Knit 2, slip 1 as if to purl, (knit 5, slip 1) 2 times, knit 2.

Row 2 (orange): Knit and purl into the first stitch and the last stitch. Purl all of the remaining knit stitches of the previous row and slip all of the slip stitches. (19 stitches)

Row 3 (brown): Slip 1 as if to purl, (knit 5, slip 1 as if to purl) 3 times.

Row 4 (brown): Slip 1 as if to purl, (knit 5, wool forward, slip 1 as if to purl, wool back) 3 times.

Row 5 (orange): Knit into the front and the back of the first stitch, knit 2, slip 1 as if to purl, (knit 5, slip 1 as if to purl) 2 times, knit 2, knit into the front and the back of the last stitch. (21 stitches)

Row 6 (orange): Knit and purl into the first stitch and the last stitch. Purl all of the remaining knit stitches of the previous row and slip all of the slip stitches. (23 stitches)

Row 7 (brown): Knit 2, slip 1 as if to purl, (knit 5, slip 1 as if to purl) 3 times, knit 2.

Row 8 (brown): Knit into the front and the back of the first stitch, knit 1, slip 1 as if to purl, (knit 5, wool forward, slip 1 as if to purl, wool back) 3 times, knit 1, knit into the front and the back of the last stitch. (25 stitches)

Row 9 (orange): Slip 1 as if to purl, (knit 5, slip 1 as if to purl) 4 times.

Row 10 (orange): Purl all of the knit stitches of the previous row and slip all of the slip stitches.

Row 11 (brown): Knit into the front and the back of the first stitch, knit 2, slip 1 as if to purl, (knit 5, slip 1) 3 times, knit 2, knit into the front and the back of the last stitch. (27 stitches)

Row 12 (brown): Knit into the front and the back of the first stitch, knit 3, wool forward, slip 1 as if to purl, wool back, (knit 5, wool forward, slip 1 as if to purl, wool back) 3 times, knit 3, knit into the front and the back of the last stitch. (29 stitches)

Row 13 (orange): Knit into the front and the back of the first stitch, knit 1, slip 1 as if to purl, (knit 5, slip 1 as if to purl) 4 times, knit 1, knit into the front and the back of the last stitch. (31 stitches)

Row 14 (orange): Knit and purl into the first stitch and the last stitch. Purl all of the remaining knit stitches of the previous row and slip all of the slip stitches. (33 stitches)

Row 15 (brown): Knit 1, slip 1 as if to purl, (knit 5, slip 1 as if to purl) 5 times, knit 1.

Row 16 (brown): Knit 1, wool forward, slip 1 as if to purl, wool back, (knit 5, wool forward, slip 1 as if to purl, wool back) 5 times, knit 1.

Row 17 (orange): Knit into the front and the back of the first stitch, knit 3, slip 1 as if to purl, (knit 5, slip 1 as if to purl) 4 times, knit 3, knit into the front and the back of the last stitch. (35 stitches)

Row 18 (orange): Purl all of the knit stitches of the previous row and slip all of the slip stitches.

Row 19 (brown): Knit into the front and the back of the first stitch, knit 1, slip 1 as if to purl, (knit 5, slip 1 as if to purl) 5 times, knit 1, knit into the front and the back of the last stitch. (37 stitches)

Row 20 (brown): Knit into the front and the back of the first stitch, knit 2, wool forward, slip 1 as if to purl, wool back, (knit 5, wool forward, slip 1 as if to purl, wool back) 5 times, knit 2, knit into the front and the back of the last stitch. (39 stitches)

Row 21 (orange): Knit into the front and the back of the first stitch, slip 1 as if to purl, (knit 5, slip 1 as if to purl) 6 times, knit into the front and the back of the last stitch. (41 stitches)

Row 22 (orange): Knit and purl into the first stitch and the last stitch. Purl all of the remaining knit stitches of the previous row and slip all of the slip stitches. (43 stitches)

Row 23 (brown): Slip 1 as if to purl, (knit 5, slip 1 as if to purl) 7 times.

Row 24 (brown): Slip 1 as if to purl, (knit 5, wool forward, slip 1 as if to purl, wool back) 7 times.

Row 25 (orange): Knit into the front and the back of the first stitch, knit 2, slip 1 as if to purl, (knit 5, slip 1 as if to purl) 6 times, knit 2, knit into the front and the back of the last stitch. (45 stitches)

Row 26 (orange): Purl all of the knit stitches of the previous row and slip all of the slip stitches.

Row 27 (brown): Knit 1, slip as if to purl, (knit 5, slip 1 as if to purl) 7 times, knit 1.

Row 28 (brown): Knit 1, wool forward, slip 1 as if to purl, wool back, (knit 5, wool forward, slip 1 as if to purl, wool back) 7 times, knit 1.

Row 29 (orange): Knit into the front and the back of the first stitch, knit 3, slip 1 as if to purl, (knit 5, slip 1 as if to purl) 6 times, knit 3, knit into the front and the back of the last stitch. (47 stitches)

Row 30 (orange): Purl all of the knit stitches of the previous row and slip all of the slip stitches.

Row 31 (brown): Knit 2, slip 1 as if to purl, (knit 5, slip 1 as if to purl) 7 times, knit 2.

Row 32 (brown): Knit 2, wool forward, slip 1 as if to purl, wool back, (knit 5, wool forward, slip 1 as if to purl, wool back) 7 times, knit 2.

Row 33 (orange): (Knit 5, slip 1 as if to purl) 7 times, knit 5.

Row 34 (orange): Repeat row 30.
Row 35 (brown): Repeat row 31.
Row 36 (brown): Repeat row 32.
Row 37 (orange): Repeat row 33.
Row 38 (orange): Repeat row 30.
Row 39 (brown): Repeat row 31.
Row 40 (brown): Repeat row 32.
Row 41 (orange): Repeat row 33.
Row 42 (orange): Repeat row 30.

Row 43 (brown): Knit into the front and the back of the first stitch, knit 1, slip 1 as if to purl, (knit 5, slip 1 as if to purl) 7 times, knit 1, knit into the front and the back of the last stitch. (49 stitches)

Row 44 (brown): Knit into the front and the back of the first stitch, knit 2, wool forward, slip 1 as if to purl, wool back, (knit 5, wool forward, slip 1 as if to purl, wool back) 7 times, knit 2, knit into the front and the back of the last stitch. (51 stitches)

Row 45 (orange): Knit into the front and the back of the first stitch, slip 1 as if to purl, (knit 5, slip 1 as if to purl) 8 times, knit into the front and the back of the last stitch. (53 stitches)

Row 46 (orange): Purl all of the knit stitches of the previous row and slip all of the slip stitches.

Row 47 (brown): (Knit 5, slip 1 as if to purl) 8 times, knit 5.

Row 48 (brown): (Knit 5, wool forward, slip 1 as if to purl, wool back) 8 times, knit 5.

Row 49 (orange): Knit 2, slip 1 as if to purl, (knit 5, slip 1 as if to purl) 8 times, knit 2.

Row 50 (orange): Purl all of the knit stitches of the previous row and slip all of the slip stitches.

Row 51 (brown): Repeat row 47.
Row 52 (brown): Repeat row 48.

Row 53 (orange): Knit into the front and the back of the first stitch, knit 1, slip 1 as if to purl, (knit 5, slip 1 as if to purl) 8 times, knit 1, knit into the front and the back of the last stitch. (55 stitches)

Row 54 (orange): Purl all of the knit stitches of the previous row and slip all of the slip stitches.

Row 55 (brown): Slip 1 as if to purl, (knit 5, slip 1 as if to purl) 9 times.

Row 56 (brown): Wool forward, slip 1 as if to purl, wool back, (knit 5, wool forward, slip 1 as if to purl, wool back) 9 times.

Row 57 (orange): Knit 3, slip 1 as if to purl, (knit 5, slip 1 as if to purl) 8 times, knit 3.

Row 58 (orange): Purl all of the knit stitches of the previous row and slip all of the slip stitches.

Rows 59, 63, 67, 71, 75, 79, 83 and 87 (brown): Repeat row 55.

Rows 60, 64, 68, 72, 76, 80, 84 and 88 (brown): Repeat row 56.

Rows 61, 65, 69, 73, 77, 81, 85 and 89 (orange): Repeat row 57.

Rows 62, 66, 70, 74, 78, 82, 86 and 90 (orange): Repeat row 58.

Row 91 (brown): Slip 1 as if to purl, (knit 5, slip 1 as if to purl) 9 times.

Row 92 (brown): Wool forward, slip 1 as if to purl, wool back, (knit 5, wool forward, slip 1 as if to purl, wool back) 9 times.

Row 93 (orange): Knit 2 together, knit 1, slip 1 as if to purl, (knit 5, slip 1 as if to purl) 8 times, knit 2 together, knit 1. (53 stitches)

Row 94 (orange): Purl all of the knit stitches of the previous row and slip all of the slip stitches.

Row 95 (brown): (Knit 5, slip 1 as if to purl) 8 times, knit 5.

Row 96 (brown): (Knit 5, wool forward, slip 1 as if to purl, wool back) 8 times, knit 5.

Row 97 (orange): Knit 2 together, slip 1 as if to purl, (knit 5, slip 1 as if to purl) 8 times, knit 2 together. (51 stitches)

Row 98 (orange): Purl all of the knit stitches of the previous row and slip all of the slip stitches.

Row 99 (brown): Knit 4, slip 1 as if to purl, (knit 5, slip 1 as if to purl) 7 times, knit 4.

Row 100 (brown): Knit 4, wool forward, slip 1 as if to purl, wool back, (knit 5, wool forward, slip 1 as if to purl, wool back) 7 times, knit 4.

Row 101 (orange): Knit 1, slip 1 as if to purl, (knit 5, slip 1 as if to purl) 8 times, knit 1.

Row 102 (orange): Purl all of the knit stitches of the previous row and slip all of the slip stitches.

Row 103 (brown): Knit 2 together, knit 2, slip 1 as if to purl, (knit 5, slip 1 as if to purl) 7 times, knit 2, knit 2 together. (49 stitches)

Row 104 (brown): Knit 2 together, knit 1, wool forward, slip 1 as if to purl, wool back, (knit 5, wool forward, slip 1 as if to purl, wool back) 7 times, knit 1, knit 2 together. (47 stitches)

Row 105 (orange): (Knit 5, slip 1 as if to purl) 7 times, knit 5.

Row 106 (orange): Purl all of the knit stitches of the previous row and slip all of the slip stitches.

Row 107 (brown): Knit 2 together, slip 1 as if to purl, (knit 5, slip 1 as if to purl) 7 times, knit 2 together. (45 stitches)

Row 108 (brown): Knit 1, wool forward, slip 1 as if to purl, wool back, (knit 5, wool forward, slip 1 as if to purl, wool back) 7 times, knit 1.

Row 109 (orange): Knit 2 together, knit 2, slip 1 as if to purl, (knit 5, slip 1 as if to purl) 6 times, knit 2, knit 2 together. (43 stitches)

Row 110 (orange): Purl all of the knit stitches of the previous row and slip all of the slip stitches.

Row 111 (brown): Knit 2 together, knit 4, slip 1 as if to purl, (knit 5, slip 1 as if to purl) 5 times, knit 4, knit 2 together. (41 stitches)

Row 112 (brown): (Knit 5, wool forward, slip 1 as if to purl, wool back) 6 times, knit 5.

Row 113 (orange): Knit 2, slip 1 as if to purl, (knit 5, slip 1 as if to purl) 6 times, knit 2.

Row 114 (orange): Purl all of the knit stitches of the previous row and slip all of the slip stitches.

Row 115 (brown): (Knit 5, slip 1 as if to purl) 6 times, knit 5.

Row 116 (brown): Repeat row 112.

Row 117 (orange): Repeat row 113.

Row 118 (orange): Repeat row 114.

Row 119 (brown): Knit 2 together, knit 3, slip 1 as if to purl, (knit 5, slip 1 as if to purl) 5 times, knit 3, knit 2 together. (39 stitches)

Row 120 (brown): Knit 2 together, knit 2, wool forward, slip 1 as if to purl, wool back, (knit 5, wool forward, slip 1 as if to purl, wool back) 5 times, knit 2, knit 2 together. (37 stitches)

Row 121 (orange): Knit 2 together, knit 4, slip 1 as if to purl, (knit 5, slip 1 as if to purl) 4 times, knit 4, knit 2 together. (35 stitches)

Row 122 (orange): Purl all of the knit stitches of the previous row and slip all of the slip stitches.
Bind off with brown.

Seat Cover Facing

DIRECTIONS: With brown, cast on 2 stitches.

Row 1 (brown): (Knit into the front and the back of the stitch) 2 times. Attach orange. The color not in use is left at the side; do not carry it across the row. (4 stitches)

Row 2 (orange): Knit into the front and the back of the first stitch, knit 2, knit into the front and the back of the last stitch. (6 stitches)

Row 3 (orange): Knit into the front and the back of the first stitch, knit 4, knit into the front and the back of the last stitch. (8 stitches)

Row 4 (brown): Knit 1, knit into the front and the back of the stitch, yarn over, knit 2 together, knit 2, knit 2 together. (8 stitches)

Row 5 (brown): Knit. (8 stitches)

Row 6 (orange): Knit 1, knit into the front and the back of the stitch, yarn over, knit 2 together, knit 2, knit 2 together. (8 stitches)

Row 7 (orange): Purl. (8 stitches)

Repeat rows 4, 5, 6 and 7 until the facing is about 1″ (2.5cm) less than the length necessary to fit around the seat cover top, ending with row 7. Then work the following 2 rows:

Row 1 (brown): Knit 2 together, knit 4, knit 2 together. (6 stitches)

Row 2 (brown): Knit 2 together, knit 2, knit 2 together. (4 stitches)
Bind off.

FINISHING: Finish following the suggestions in the "Hints on Finishing" section in the appendix. Join the seat cover facing to the seat cover top, keeping the beading (the yarn overs) to the inside. Weave a strand of yarn through the beading and adjust to fit around the toilet seat.

TOILET TISSUE COVER

MATERIALS: One 80-yard (73m) skein yellow Lily Rug Yarn, one 80-yard (73m) skein orange Lily Rug Yarn, size 9 double-pointed knitting needles (set of four), 1/2'' (13mm) elastic, large-eyed tapestry needle.

NOTE: Always mark the start of each round by placing a safety pin in the first stitch of the round. Move the pin when you reach this stitch and replace it in the new stitch just formed.

DIRECTIONS: With orange, cast 54 stitches onto one double-pointed needle. Divide the stitches evenly onto three needles; join, being careful not to twist the stitches.

Sides

Round 1 (orange): Knit.
Round 2 (orange): Knit. Attach yellow. The color not in use is left at the side; do not carry it around the round.
Round 3 (yellow): *Knit 2, slip 1 as if to purl, knit 5.* Repeat from * to * around the round to the last 4 stitches. Slip 1 as if to purl, knit 3.
Round 4 (yellow): Repeat round 3.
Round 5 (orange): *Knit 5, slip 1 as if to purl.* Repeat from * to * around the round.

Round 6 (orange): *Purl 5, wool back, slip 1 as if to purl, wool forward.* Repeat from * to * around the round.
Repeat rows 3, 4, 5 and 6 eight times, or until the sides are the desired height, ending with row 6.

Top

DIRECTIONS: Continue working with the stitches on the three needles.
Round 1 (yellow): *Knit 2, slip 1 as if to purl, knit 5.* Repeat from * to * around the round to the last 4 stitches. Slip 1 as if to purl, knit 3.
Round 2 (yellow): Knit 2, slip 1 as if to purl, knit 5, slip 1 as if to purl, (knit 2 together, knit 3, slip 1 as if to purl) 6 times, knit 5, slip 1 as if to purl, knit 3. (48 stitches)
Round 3 (orange): Knit 5, slip 1 as if to purl, (knit 4, slip 1 as if to purl) 6 times, (knit 5, slip 1 as if to purl) 2 times.
Round 4 (orange): Purl 5, wool back, slip 1 as if to purl, wool forward, (purl 2 together, purl 2, wool back, slip 1 as if to purl, wool forward) 6 times, (purl 5, wool back, slip 1 as if to purl, wool forward) 2 times. (42 stitches)

Round 5 (yellow): Knit 2, slip 1 as if to purl, knit 4, slip 1 as if to purl, (knit 3, slip 1 as if to purl) 5 times, knit 4, slip 1 as if to purl, knit 5, slip 1 as if to purl, knit 3.

Round 6 (yellow): Knit 2 together, slip 1 as if to purl, knit 2 together, knit 2, slip 1 as if to purl, (knit 3, slip 1 as if to purl) 5 times, knit 2, knit 2 together, slip 1 as if to purl, knit 2 together, knit 1, knit 2 together, slip 1 as if to purl, knit 2 together, knit 1. (36 stitches)

Round 7 (orange): *Knit 3, slip 1 as if to purl.* Repeat from * to * around the round.

Round 8 (orange): (Purl 3, wool back, slip 1 as if to purl, wool forward) 2 times, (purl 2 together, purl 1, wool back, slip 1 as if to purl, wool forward) 6 times, purl 3, wool back, slip 1 as if to purl, wool forward. (30 stitches)

Round 9 (yellow): Knit 1, slip 1 as if to purl, knit 3, slip 1 as if to purl, (knit 2, slip 1 as if to purl) 6 times, knit 3, slip 1 as if to purl, knit 2.

Round 10 (yellow): Knit 1, slip 1 as if to purl, knit 2 together, knit 1, slip 1 as if to purl, (knit 2, slip 1 as if to purl) 6 times, knit 2 together, knit 1, slip 1 as if to purl, knit 2 together. (27 stitches)

Round 11 (orange): Knit 2 together, slip 1 as if to purl, knit 2 together, knit 1, slip 1 as if to purl, (knit 2 together, slip 1 as if to purl) 6 times, knit 1, slip 1 as if to purl. (19 stitches)

Round 12 (orange): Purl 1, wool back, slip 1 as if to purl, wool forward, purl 2, wool back, slip 1 as if to purl, wool forward, (purl 1, wool back, slip 1 as if to purl, wool forward) 7 times.

Round 13 (yellow): Knit.

Round 14 (yellow): *Knit 1, knit 2 together.* Repeat from * to * around the round to the last stitch. Knit 1. (13 stitches)

Round 15 (orange): (Knit 2, knit 2 together) 2 times, (knit 2 together) 2 times, knit 1. (9 stitches)

Round 16 (orange): Purl.

Cut the threads, leaving an 8'' (20.5cm) end on the orange thread. Draw this end through the remaining 9 stitches and tie. Weave the yellow thread through the back.

FINISHING: Finish following the suggestions in the "Hints on Finishing" section in the appendix. Following the instructions in the appendix, make a ball, using strands of both yellow and orange. Use two circles of cardboard, each 3'' (7.5cm) in diameter. Cut a smaller circle out of the center of each, leaving about 3/4'' (20mm) of the outer circle. Sew this ball on top of the toilet tissue cover. If necessary, attach elastic around the bottom of the cover and adjust to fit.

TISSUE BOX COVER

SIZE: Standard tissue box.

MATERIALS: One 80-yard (73m) skein yellow Lily Rug Yarn, one 80-yard (73m) skein orange Lily Rug Yarn, size 9 knitting needles, 1/2'' (13mm) elastic.

DIRECTIONS: With orange, cast on 30 stitches.

Row 1 (orange): Knit.

Row 2 (orange): Knit. Attach yellow. The color not in use is left at the side; do not carry it across the row.

Row 3 (yellow): Knit 2, (slip 1 as if to purl, knit 5) 4 times, slip 1 as if to purl, knit 3.

Row 4 (yellow): Purl all of the knit stitches of the previous row and slip all of the slip stitches.

Row 5 (orange): (Knit 5, slip 1 as if to purl) 5 times.

Row 6 (orange): (Wool forward, slip 1 as if to purl, wool back, knit 5) 5 times.

Rows 7, 11, 15 and 19 (yellow): Repeat row 3.

Rows 8, 12, 16 and 20 (yellow): Repeat row 4.

Rows 9, 13, 17 and 21 (orange): Repeat row 5.

Rows 10, 14, 18 and 22 (orange): Repeat row 6.

Row 23 (yellow): Repeat row 3.

Row 24 (yellow): Repeat row 4. Cut yellow thread.

Row 25 (orange): Cast on 14 stitches at the beginning of the row and work across the entire row in this manner: Knit 1, slip 1 as if to purl, (knit 5, slip 1 as if to purl) 7 times. (44 stitches)

Row 26 (orange): Cast on 14 stitches at the beginning of the row and work across the entire row in this manner: Knit 2, wool forward, slip 1 as if to purl, wool back, (knit 5, wool forward, slip 1 as if to purl, wool back) 9 times, knit 1. Attach yellow thread. (58 stitches)

Row 27 (yellow): Knit 4, (Slip 1 as if to purl, knit 5) 9 times.

Row 28 (yellow): Purl all of the knit stitches of the previous row and slip all of the slip stitches.

Row 29 (orange): Knit 1, slip 1 as if to purl, (knit 5, slip 1 as if to purl) 9 times, knit 2.

Row 30 (orange): Knit 2, wool forward, slip 1 as if to purl, wool back, (knit 5, wool forward, slip 1 as if to purl, wool back) 9 times, knit 1.

Row 31 (yellow): Repeat row 27.

Row 32 (yellow): Repeat row 28.

Row 33 (orange): Repeat row 29.

Row 34 (orange): Repeat row 30.

Row 35 (yellow): Repeat row 27.

Row 36 (yellow): Repeat row 28.

Row 37 (orange): Repeat row 29.
Row 38 (orange): Repeat row 30.
Row 39 (yellow): Repeat row 27.
Row 40 (yellow): Repeat row 28.
Row 41 (orange): Knit 1, slip 1 as if to purl, (knit 5, slip 1 as if to purl) 2 times, knit 1. Bind off 28 stitches. (Knit 5, slip 1 as if to purl) 2 times, knit 3. (30 stitches)
Row 42 (orange): Knit 3, (wool forward, slip 1 as if to purl, wool back, knit 5) 2 times. Cast on 28 stitches. Knit 1, (wool forward, slip 1 as if to purl, wool back, knit 5) 2 times, wool forward, slip 1 as if to purl, wool back, knit 1. (58 stitches)
Row 43 (yellow): Knit 4, (slip 1 as if to purl, knit 5) 9 times.
Row 44 (yellow): Purl all of the knit stitches of the previous row and slip all of the slip stitches.
Row 45 (orange): Knit 1, slip 1 as if to purl, (knit 5, slip 1 as if to purl) 9 times, knit 2.
Row 46 (orange): Knit 2, wool forward, slip 1 as if to purl, wool back, (knit 5, wool forward, slip 1 as if to purl, wool back) 9 times, knit 1.
Row 47 (yellow): Repeat row 43.
Row 48 (yellow): Repeat row 44.
Row 49 (orange): Repeat row 45.
Row 50 (orange): Repeat row 46.
Row 51 (yellow): Repeat row 43.
Row 52 (yellow): Repeat row 44.
Row 53 (orange): Repeat row 45.
Row 54 (orange): Repeat row 46.
Row 55 (yellow): Repeat row 43.
Row 56 (yellow): Repeat row 44. Cut yellow thread.
Row 57 (orange): Repeat row 45.
Row 58 (orange): Bind off 14 stitches. (Wool forward, slip 1 as if to purl, wool back, knit 5) 5 times. Bind off 14 stitches. Cut orange thread and attach yellow thread. (30 stitches)
Row 59 (yellow): Knit 2, (slip 1 as if to purl, knit 5) 4 times, slip 1 as if to purl, knit 3.
Row 60 (yellow): Purl all of the knit stitches of the previous row and slip all of the slip stitches. Attach orange thread.

Row 61 (orange): (Knit 5, slip 1 as if to purl) 5 times.
Row 62 (orange): (Wool forward, slip 1 as if to purl, wool back, knit 5) 5 times.
Row 63 (yellow): Knit 2, (slip 1 as if to purl, knit 5) 4 times, slip 1 as if to purl, knit 3.
Row 64 (yellow): Purl all of the knit stitches of the previous row and slip all of the slip stitches.
Row 65 (orange): Repeat row 61.
Row 66 (orange): Repeat row 62.
Row 67 (yellow): Repeat row 63.
Row 68 (yellow): Repeat row 64.
Row 69 (orange): Repeat row 61.
Row 70 (orange): Repeat row 62.
Row 71 (yellow): Repeat row 63.
Row 72 (yellow): Repeat row 64.
Row 73 (orange): Repeat row 61.
Row 74 (orange): Repeat row 62.
Row 75 (yellow): Repeat row 63.
Row 76 (yellow): Repeat row 64.
Row 77 (orange): Repeat row 61.
Row 78 (orange): Repeat row 62.
Row 79 (yellow): Repeat row 63.
Row 80 (orange): Repeat row 64.
Row 81 (orange): Knit.
Bind off with orange.

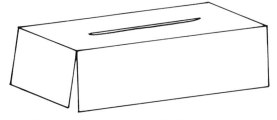

Joining the Four Corners of the Tissue Box Cover

FINISHING: Finish following the suggestions in the "Hints on Finishing" section in the appendix. Join the edges at each corner, as shown in the diagram. Sew elastic around the bottom and adjust to fit.

7.

THE BEDROOM

Children will have their way! No matter how hard I tried, I never could convince my children to "play in your room." When I decorated their bedrooms I followed the suggestions of the best contemporary sources. The walls were lined with toy shelves, toy chests, charming pictures, and delightful books. I tried to make their rooms as pleasant as possible so that they'd "play in your room" and give the rest of the house (and a tired mommy) a break. They played in their rooms only while I made the beds. No matter what I did—cajoled, begged, threatened, screamed— they preferred playing under my feet. By the time the third child arrived, I had decided that the ideal house would be one with monks' cells for bedrooms and one huge room where mommy spent her spare time in company with the kids.

This stopped, as if by magic, the year each one, in turn, became a teen-ager. Suddenly a bedroom became sacrosanct. Now, not only did they never leave the room, but no one else was permitted to enter the inner sanctum. Suddenly the bedroom became terribly important—not for cleaning, of course, but for living. Since I am no longer permitted to enter teen-agers' rooms (except by invitation once every Fourth of July), the cry in our house is no longer, "play in your room" but "clean your room!"

We are very fortunate that each child has been able to have her own room. I've always sympathized with the desire of anyone to have a place of his or her own, especially during the teen years, when a bedroom must reflect one's personality. I've therefore permitted each of my daughters to decorate her own room. One is a traditionalist; her bedroom looks like something out of the last century. Another is a very serious young lady who has a bedroom that looks like a study-library. The third daughter, who is very "with it," has a bedroom decorated with posters advertising the latest rock stars. Notice, no knitting can be found!

There is something about the warmth and comfort of a knitted piece that adds not only beauty but a certain character to a room, but I've had to reserve my bedroom knitting for our guest room. Many of the pieces that appear in this book—rugs, doilies, curtains, afghans, pillows—are duplicated in my guest bedroom. I will not repeat them here. The one project that appears in this chapter is the project I have made solely for my guest bedroom, and which enjoys a place of honor there: the "Log Cabin Patchwork Quilt". It never fails to receive the proper "oohs" and "aahs" from my guests, who can't help but feel pampered to find such a beautiful piece of knitting waiting for them.

LOG CABIN PATCHWORK QUILT

If you have made cloth patchwork quilts, or if you have admired antique patchwork quilts in shops or in books, you will enjoy *knitting* a patchwork quilt. The knitted quilt is made in much the same manner as a real patchwork quilt. Small squares are made and then joined to create a design. Sometimes the individual squares seem to bear no relationship to the finished design, but once they are all joined the design will appear.

Each block must be a square; the blocks in my quilt are 8'' x 8'' (20.5cm x 20.5cm). In order to get an 8'' x 8'' square, I followed a gauge of 9 stitches = 2'' (5cm) and 11 rows = 2'' (5cm). You can use your own gauge as long as your blocks end up being squares.

The blocks are worked with bobbins of each color, and the colors are alternately picked up and dropped; the colors are not carried across the back of the work. You can work with small balls or even skeins, but the bobbins are easier to work with because they are smaller and easier to manipulate. In the appendix, I've given you some suggestions on knitting with colors as well as a pattern for making your own bobbins. You can use the colors

I have suggested, or you can use up scraps of wool left over from other projects so long as you use two dark colors, two light colors, and one very light color for each block.

An Individual Block

You will have to make two different squares—one a mirror image of the other. To make a patchwork quilt that is approximately the same size as mine, make twenty-four "A" blocks and twenty-four "B" blocks. To make a larger quilt, make more squares, but always make an even number of "A" and "B" blocks.

In addition to the two designs shown here, many other versions of the log cabin quilt can be made with the same squares. By arranging the forty-eight squares in different formations, you can create some of these traditional patterns.

By the way, if you don't want to put your quilt on a bed, you can follow the lead of many current quilt collectors. You can hang your knitted log cabin patchwork quilt on the wall. It makes a beautiful wall hanging.

SIZE: Approximately 48″ x 64″ (122cm x 162.5cm).

MATERIALS: 20 ounces purple four-ply knitting worsted, 20 ounces blue four-ply knitting worsted, 20 ounces pink four-ply knitting worsted, 20 ounces orange four-ply knitting worsted, 4 ounces pale yellow four-ply knitting worsted, size 7 knitting needles, 9 bobbins, large-eyed tapestry needle, lining fabric.

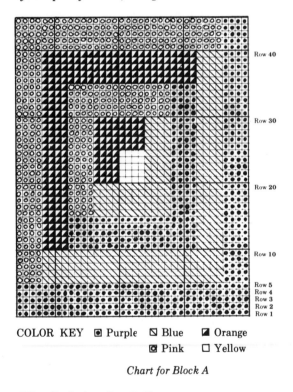

COLOR KEY   ▣ Purple   ◨ Blue   ◪ Orange
                          ▣ Pink   ☐ Yellow

Chart for Block A

Block A (make 24)

DIRECTIONS: Wind the following bobbins: 2 purple, 2 blue, 2 pink, 2 orange, 1 pale yellow. With purple, cast on 36 stitches.

NOTE: When making color changes, twist the yarn once and bring the new color from underneath the old color to avoid holes.

Rows 1, 3 and 5: Knit 36 purple.

Rows 2 and 4: Purl 36 purple.

Rows 6, 8 and 10: Purl 4 pink, 28 blue, 4 purple.

Rows 7 and 9: Knit 4 purple, 28 blue, 4 pink.

Rows 11, 13 and 15: Knit 4 purple, 4 blue, 20 purple, 4 orange, 4 pink.

Rows 12 and 14: Purl 4 pink, 4 orange, 20 purple, 4 blue, 4 purple.

Rows 16, 18 and 20: Purl 4 pink, 4 orange, 4 pink, 12 blue, 4 purple, 4 blue, 4 purple.

Rows 17 and 19: Knit 4 purple, 4 blue, 4 purple, 12 blue, 4 pink, 4 orange, 4 pink.

Rows 21, 23 and 25: Knit 4 purple, 4 blue, 4 purple, 4 blue, 4 yellow, 4 orange, 4 pink, 4 orange, 4 pink.

Rows 22 and 24: Purl 4 pink, 4 orange, 4 pink, 4 orange, 4 yellow, 4 blue, 4 purple, 4 blue, 4 purple.

Rows 26, 28 and 30: Purl 4 pink, 4 orange, 4 pink, 8 orange, 4 blue, 4 purple, 4 blue, 4 purple.

Rows 27 and 29: Knit 4 purple, 4 blue, 4 purple, 4 blue, 8 orange, 4 pink, 4 orange, 4 pink.

Rows 31, 33 and 35: Knit 4 purple, 4 blue, 4 purple, 16 pink, 4 orange, 4 pink.

Rows 32 and 34: Purl 4 pink, 4 orange, 16 pink, 4 purple, 4 blue, 4 purple.

Rows 36, 38 and 40: Purl 4 pink, 24 orange, 4 blue, 4 purple.

Rows 37 and 39: Knit 4 purple, 4 blue, 24 orange, 4 pink.

Rows 41, 43 and 45: Knit 4 purple, 32 pink.

Rows 42 and 44: Purl 32 pink, 4 purple.
Bind off.

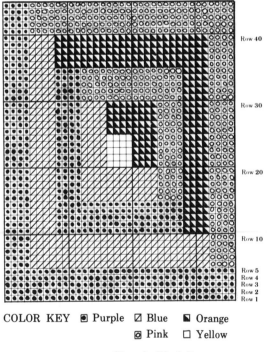

COLOR KEY   ▣ Purple   ◨ Blue   ◪ Orange
                          ▣ Pink   ☐ Yellow

Chart for Block B

Block B (make 24)

DIRECTIONS: Wind the following bobbins: 2 purple, 2

blue, 2 pink, 2 orange, 1 pale yellow. With purple, cast on 36 stitches.

NOTE: When making color changes, twist the yarn once and bring the new color from underneath the old color to avoid holes.

Rows 1, 3 and 5: Knit 36 purple.
Rows 2 and 4: Purl 36 purple.
Rows 6, 8 and 10: Purl 4 purple, 28 blue, 4 pink.
Rows 7 and 9: Knit 4 pink, 28 blue, 4 purple.
Rows 11, 13 and 15: Knit 4 pink, 4 orange, 20 purple, 4 blue, 4 purple.
Rows 12 and 14: Purl 4 purple, 4 blue, 20 purple, 4 orange, 4 pink.
Rows 16, 18 and 20: Purl 4 purple, 4 blue, 4 purple, 12 blue, 4 pink, 4 orange, 4 pink.
Rows 17 and 19: Knit 4 pink, 4 orange, 4 pink, 12 blue, 4 purple, 4 blue, 4 purple.
Rows 21, 23 and 25: Knit 4 pink, 4 orange, 4 pink, 4 orange, 4 yellow, 4 blue, 4 purple, 4 blue, 4 purple.
Rows 22 and 24: Purl 4 purple, 4 blue, 4 purple, 4 blue, 4 yellow, 4 orange, 4 pink, 4 orange, 4 pink.
Rows 26, 28 and 30: Purl 4 purple, 4 blue, 4 purple, 4 blue, 8 orange, 4 pink, 4 orange, 4 pink.
Rows 27 and 29: Knit 4 pink, 4 orange, 4 pink, 8 orange, 4 blue, 4 purple, 4 blue, 4 purple.
Rows 31, 33 and 35: Knit 4 pink, 4 orange, 16 pink, 4 purple, 4 blue, 4 purple.
Rows 32 and 34: Purl 4 purple, 4 blue, 4 purple, 16 pink, 4 orange, 4 pink.
Rows 36, 38 and 40: Purl 4 purple, 4 blue, 24 orange, 4 pink.

Rows 37 and 39: Knit 4 pink, 24 orange, 4 blue, 4 purple.
Rows 41, 43 and 45: Knit 32 pink, 4 purple.
Rows 42 and 44: Purl 4 purple, 32 pink.
Bind off.

FINISHING: Thread the ends through the tapestry needle and weave into the back of each block. With a warm steam iron, carefully block each square. Following the diagram for the completed quilt (first or second versions), join the squares, using either Block "A" or Block "B" as needed.

Measure the completed quilt top and cut the lining fabric so that it is 2″ longer and 2″ wider than the quilt top. Fold under 1″ on each side. Lay the lining fabric wrong side up on a large, flat surface. Place the quilt on the lining fabric, wrong sides together. Starting with one of the short sides, begin to baste the quilt top to the lining fabric. Then work down one long side, do the other short side and the remaining long side last. Do not stretch the quilt top.

"Tie" the quilt top to the lining at the middle and corners of each square. To do this, thread the tapestry needle with yarn in either a matching or contrasting color; do not knot the thread. Pass the yarn from the knitted top through both the knitted quilt top and the lining fabric, leaving about 1″ (2.5cm) of yarn on the knitted side. Bring the needle back up from the bottom to the top and tie the yarn in a knot, leaving ends about 1/2″ (1.3cm) long. Cut both yarn ends to the same length.
Blanket stitch around the four edges.

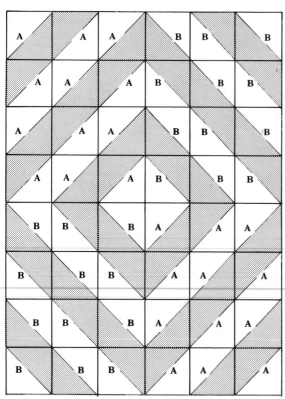

Diagram for the Completed Quilt (First Version)

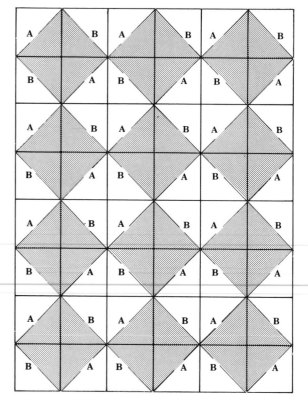

Diagram for the Completed Quilt (Second Version)

8.

IT'S CHRISTMAS!

If there is one time of the year when everyone's creative juices start to flow, it's Christmas! You may never needlepoint, crochet, embroider, knit, do macrame, or make things out of wood at any other time of the year, but when the Christmas carols are heard, and the stores put up their decorations, you're suddenly driven by the desire to create something.

Most craftspeople love to make ornaments for the Christmas tree. Of course, there are those who insist that handmade Christmas ornaments are just "too déclassé." And there are those who wouldn't hang anything on the Christmas tree unless it had been fashioned by hand. I think that most people fall somewhere in between; they like to have a few handmade ornaments shining through the maze of purchased trinkets.

Naturally if you're going to make ornaments for the tree, you can't decide the night before that you're going to decorate your tree with handmade ornaments. You've got to start planning a little bit before the big day. I have a friend who literally starts planning for next year's Christmas on December 26. Then I have a friend of the other type, who cries on December 24, "I really meant to get those ornaments made, but I just never had the time." The ornaments in this chapter will satisfy both of my friends. If you want to work all year making ornaments, you can make the ones in this chapter and then use these instructions as a springboard for your own creativity by designing your own versions. If you wake up on the morning of December 24 and decide that you must have something handmade for your tree, you can create at least one of these ornaments in less than a day.

All of the ornaments are actually 4 1/2″ (11.5cm) high versions of a set of knitted dolls that I made for my oldest daughter before she was born. They are all made in much the same way, but the use of different colors and the addition of embroidered faces change their personalities. Make them with bits and pieces of two-ply knitting yarn and size 3 double-pointed knitting needles. One ounce of yarn will produce enough ornaments to decorate an entire tree. If you don't want to buy new yarn, search your house for odd bits left over from other projects, especially from baby sweaters. Pieces of yarn left over from needlepoint or crewel projects can also be used.

My ornaments are always stuffed with polyester fiberfill, which is available at department and craft stores and sometimes at yard goods stores as well. It is usually sold by the pound, and a pound of fiberfill will stuff enough ornaments to decorate about ten Christmas trees. If you plan to make only a few ornaments, you might think about using other materials for stuffing. The lint collected from a clothes dryer, for example, makes excellent stuffing material, as do old cut-up nylon stockings.

When you have finished knitting and stuffing the ornaments, the faces can be embroidered like the ones in the photograph, or you can use bits of felt glued to the ornament. The faces can even be decorated with felt-tipped pens. Use your imagination! After you have completed each ornament, attach a string for hanging. You may have to experiment a bit to get the string attached in just the right place so that the ornament will hang correctly.

One year I made a batch of these ornaments and sent them as Christmas cards. They met with such acclaim that the next year I stopped sending Christmas cards because I just couldn't top the high of the previous year. Be careful, therefore, if you make these ornaments for gifts or to sell at your church bazaar; you might find yourself in the ornament-making business for the remainder of the year and part of the next.

Christmas Ornaments. *(top row) Angel, (middle row, left to right) Snowman, Santa Claus, Santa's Elf. (bottom row, left to right) Clown, Choir Boy.*

SANTA CLAUS ORNAMENT

MATERIALS: Small amounts of red, white, black and pink two-ply knitting yarn, size 3 double-pointed knitting needles (set of four), stuffing material, large-eyed tapestry needle.

Right Leg

DIRECTIONS: Work in rows with two double-pointed knitting needles. With black, cast 12 stitches onto one double-pointed needle.

Row 1: Purl.

Row 2: Knit.

Row 3: Purl 6, (purl 2 together) 2 times, purl 2. (10 stitches)

Row 4: Knit 1, (knit 2 together) 2 times, knit 5. Cut black; attach red. (8 stitches)

Rows 5 and 7: Purl.

Rows 6 and 8: Knit.

Row 9: Purl. Cut red yarn; leave the stitches on the double-pointed needle and set aside to be worked later.

Left Leg

DIRECTIONS: Work in rows with two double-pointed knitting needles. With black, cast 12 stitches onto one double-pointed needle.

Row 1: Purl.

Row 2: Knit.

Row 3: Purl 2, (purl 2 together) 2 times, purl 6. (10 stitches)

Row 4: Knit 5, (knit 2 together) 2 times, knit 1. Cut black; attach red. (8 stitches)

Rows 5, 7 and 9: Purl.

Rows 6 and 8: Knit.

Join legs: Working from the right side, knit across the first 4 stitches of the left leg, which are on the needle (this will become the first needle). Knit the remaining 4 stitches of the left leg and the first 4 stitches of the right leg onto the second double-pointed needle; this will become the front of the body. With the third double-pointed needle, knit the remaining 4 stitches of the right leg. Mark this last stitch with a safety pin as the end of the round; this will be the center back of the ornament.

Body

DIRECTIONS: Work in rounds with the four double-pointed knitting needles.

NOTE: Always mark the end of each round by placing a safety pin in the last stitch of the round. Move the pin when you reach this stitch and replace it in the new stitch just formed.

Round 1: Knit. (16 stitches)

Round 2: Knit 1, (knit into the front and the back of the stitch, knit 3) 3 times, knit into the front and the back of the stitch, knit 2. (20 stitches)

Round 3: Knit.

Round 4: Knit. Cut red; attach black.

Round 5: Knit.

Round 6: Knit. Cut black; attach red.

Rounds 7, 8, 9 and 10: Knit.

Round 11: Knit 2, knit 2 together, knit 12, knit 2 together, knit 2. (18 stitches)

Rounds 12 and 13: Knit.

Round 14: Knit 2, knit 2 together, knit 10, knit 2 together, knit 2. (16 stitches)

Round 15: Knit around the round, placing 4 stitches on the first needle, 8 stitches on the second needle and 4 stitches on the third needle.

Rounds 16, 17 and 18: Knit.

Round 19: *Knit 2 stitches together.* Repeat from * to * around the round. Cut red; attach pink. (8 stitches)

Head

DIRECTIONS: Continue working in rounds with the four double-pointed knitting needles.

Round 1: Knit.

Round 2: *Knit into the front and the back of the stitch.* Repeat from * to * around the round. (16 stitches)

Round 3: Knit.

Round 4: Knit 1, (knit into the front and the back of the stitch, knit 3) 3 times, knit into the front and the back of the stitch, knit 2. (20 stitches)

Rounds 5, 6 and 7: Knit.

Round 8: Knit 2, knit into the front and the back of the stitch, knit 13, knit into the front and the back of the stitch, knit 3. (22 stitches)

Rounds 9 and 10: Knit.

Round 11: Knit 2, knit 2 together, knit 14, knit 2 together, knit 2. (20 stitches)

Round 12: Knit.

Round 13: *Knit 2 together, knit 3.* Repeat from * to * around the round. (16 stitches)

Round 14: Knit.

Round 15: *Knit 2 together, knit 2.* Repeat from * to * around the round. (12 stitches)

Weaving the head: With the third needle, knit the 3 stitches from the first needle so that there are only two needles, with 6 stitches on each. Place the two needles parallel to each other. Cut the yarn, leaving an end of about 12″ (30.5cm), and thread this end into the large-eyed tapestry needle. *Insert the tapestry needle through the first stitch on the front knitting needle as if to knit and slip the stitch off the knitting needle; insert the tapestry needle through the next stitch on the front needle as if to purl, but leave the stitch on the needle; insert the tapestry needle through the first stitch on the back needle as if to purl and slip the stitch off the knitting needle; insert the tapestry needle through the next stitch on the back needle as if to knit, but leave the stitch on the needle.* Repeat from * to * until all of the stitches have been woven. Fasten off the yarn.

Arms (make 2)

DIRECTIONS: Work in rows with two double-pointed needles. With black, cast 8 stitches onto one double-pointed needle.
Row 1: Purl.
Row 2: Knit. Cut black; attach white.
Row 3: Purl.
Row 4: Knit. Cut white; attach red.
Rows 5, 7, 9, 11 and 13: Purl.
Rows 6, 8, 10 and 12: Knit.
Bind off.

HAT

DIRECTIONS: Work in rounds with four double-pointed needles. With white, cast 24 stitches onto one double-pointed needle. Divide the stitches evenly onto three needles; join, being careful not to twist the stitches.

NOTE: Always mark the start of each round by placing a safety pin in the first stitch of the round. Move the pin when you reach this stitch and replace it in the new stitch just formed.

Rounds 1, 2 and 3: *Knit 1, purl 1.* Repeat from * to * around the round. Cut white; attach red.
Rounds 4 and 5: Knit.
Round 6: Knit 2, knit 2 together, knit 16, knit 2 together, knit 3. (22 stitches)
Round 7: Knit.
Round 8: (Knit 2 together, knit 3) 4 times, knit 2. (18 stitches)
Round 9: Knit.
Round 10: (Knit 2 together, knit 2) 4 times, knit 2. (14 stitches)
Round 11: Knit.
Round 12: *Knit 2 together.* Repeat from * to * around the round. (7 stitches)
Round 13: Knit around the round, placing 2 stitches on the first needle, 3 stitches on the second needle and 2 stitches on the third needle.
Round 14: Knit.
Bind off.

FINISHING: Stuff the body and the head through the legs. Stuff very firmly. Sew the leg seams, stuffing the legs firmly as you sew. Then sew each arm together and

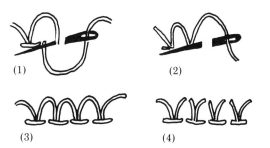

Turkey Work. (1) *Working from the bottom of the area to the top, make a stitch, pulling it tight; make another stitch, leaving a loop. Use your thumb to hold the loop while the stitch is being made.* **(2)** *Make another stitch and pull it tight; make another stitch leaving a loop. Continue in this manner until the area is covered.* **(3)** *Unclipped turkey work.* **(4)** *Clipped turkey work.*

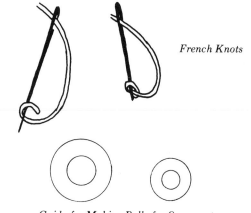

French Knots

Guide for Making Balls for Ornaments

stuff firmly. Attach the arms to the sides of the body. Make the beard and hair by working clipped turkey work around Santa Claus's face and head. Embroider the eyes and nose with large French knots. Following the instructions for making trims given in the appendix, and using the large circle as a guide, make one large white ball. Attach to the top of the hat and sew the hat to the head. Attach string for hanging.

SANTA'S ELF ORNAMENT

MATERIALS: Small amounts of green, pink, white, red and blue two-ply knitting yarn, size 3 double-pointed knitting needles (set of four), stuffing material, large-eyed tapestry needle.

Right Leg

DIRECTIONS: Work in rows with two double-pointed knitting needles. With green, cast 12 stitches onto one double-pointed needle.
Row 1: Purl.
Row 2: Knit.
Row 3: Purl 6, (purl 2 together) 2 times, purl 2. (10 stitches)

Row 4: Knit 1, (knit 2 together) 2 times, knit 5. (8 stitches)
Rows 5 and 7: Purl.
Rows 6 and 8: Knit.
Row 9: Purl. Cut yarn; leave the stitches on the double-pointed needle and set aside to be worked later.

Left Leg

DIRECTIONS: Work in rows with two double-pointed needles. With green, cast 12 stitches onto one double-pointed needle.
Row 1: Purl.
Row 2: Knit.
Row 3: Purl, (purl 2 together) 2 times, purl 6. (10 stitches)
Row 4: Knit 5, (knit 2 together) 2 times, knit 1. (8 stitches)
Rows 5, 7 and 9: Purl.
Rows 6 and 8: Knit.
Join legs: Working from the right side, knit across the first 4 stitches of the left leg, which are on the needle. (This will become the first needle.) Knit the remaining 4 stitches of the left leg and the first 4 stitches of the right leg onto the second double-pointed needle; this will become the front of the body. With the third double-pointed needle, knit the remaining 4 stitches of the right leg. Mark this last stitch as the end of the round; this will be the center back of the ornament.

Body

DIRECTIONS: Work in rounds with the four double-pointed knitting needles.

NOTE: Always mark the end of each round by placing a safety pin in the last stitch of the round. Move the pin when you reach this stitch and replace it in the new stitch just formed.

Round 1: Knit. (16 stitches)
Round 2: Knit 1, (knit into the front and the back of the stitch, knit 3) 3 times, knit into the front and the back of the stitch, knit 2. (20 stitches)
Rounds 3, 4, 5, 6, 7, 8, 9 and 10: Knit.
Round 11: Knit 2, knit 2 together, knit 12, knit 2 together, knit 2. (18 stitches)
Rounds 12 and 13: Knit.
Round 14: Knit 2, knit 2 together, knit 10, knit 2 together, knit 2. (16 stitches)
Round 15: Knit around the round, placing 4 stitches on the first needle, 8 stitches on the second needle and 4 stitches on the third needle.
Rounds 17 and 18: Knit.
Round 19: *Knit 2 together.* Repeat from * to * around the round. Cut green; attach pink. (8 stitches)

Head

DIRECTIONS: Continue working in rounds with the four double-pointed needles.
Round 1: Knit.

Round 2: *Knit into the front and the back of the stitch.* Repeat from * to * around the round. (16 stitches)
Round 3: Knit.
Round 4: Knit 1, (knit into the front and the back of the stitch, knit 3) 3 times, knit into the front and the back of the stitch, knit 2. (20 stitches)
Rounds 5, 6 and 7: Knit.
Round 8: Knit 2, knit into the front and the back of the stitch, knit 13, knit into the front and the back of the stitch, knit 3. (22 stitches)
Rounds 9 and 10: Knit.
Round 11: Knit 2, knit 2 together, knit 14, knit 2 together, knit 2. (20 stitches)
Round 12: Knit.
Round 13: *Knit 2 together, knit 3.* Repeat from * to * around the round. (16 stitches)
Round 14: Knit.
Round 15: *Knit 2 together, knit 2.* Repeat from * to * around the round. (12 stitches)
Weaving the head: With the third needle, knit the 3 stitches from the first needle so that there are only two needles, with 6 stitches on each. Place the two needles parallel to each other. Cut the yarn, leaving an end of about 12″ (30.5cm), and thread this end into the large-eyed tapestry needle. *Insert the tapestry needle through the first stitch on the front needle as if to knit and slip this stitch off the knitting needle; insert the tapestry needle through the next stitch on the front needle as if to purl, but leave the stitch on the needle; insert the tapestry needle through the first stitch on the back needle as if to purl and slip the stitch off the knitting needle; insert the tapestry needle through the next stitch on the back needle as if to knit, but leave the stitch on the needle.* Repeat from * to * until all of the stitches have been woven.
Fasten off the yarn.

Arms (make 2)

DIRECTIONS: Work in rows with two double-pointed needles. With pink, cast 8 stitches onto one double-pointed needle.
Row 1: Purl.
Row 2: Knit.
Row 3: Purl 2, (purl 2 together) 2 times, purl 2. Cut pink; attach green. (6 stitches)
Rows 4, 6, 8, 10 and 12: Knit.
Rows 5, 7, 9, 11 and 13: Purl.
Bind off.

HAT

DIRECTIONS: Work in rounds with four double-pointed needles. With green, cast 24 stitches onto one double-pointed needle. Divide the stitches evenly onto 3 needles; join, being careful not to twist the stitches.

NOTE: Always mark the start of each round by placing a safety pin in the first stitch of the round. Move the pin when you reach this stitch and replace it in the new stitch just formed.

Rounds 1, 2, 3, 4 and 5: Knit.
Round 6: Knit 2, knit 2 together, knit 16, knit 2 together, knit 2. (22 stitches)
Round 7: Knit.
Round 8: (Knit 2 together, knit 3) 4 times, knit 2. (18 stitches)
Round 9: Knit.
Round 10: (Knit 2 together, knit 2) 4 times, knit 2. (14 stitches)
Round 11: Knit around the round, placing 5 stitches on the first needle, 4 stitches on the second needle and 5 stitches on the third needle.
Round 12: Knit 1, knit 2 together, knit 8, knit 2 together, knit 1. (12 stitches)
Round 13: Knit.
Round 14: Knit 2, (knit 2 together) 4 times, knit 2. (8 stitches)
Round 15: Knit around the round, placing 2 stitches on the first needle, 4 stitches on the second needle and 2 stitches on the third needle.
Round 16: Knit 2, (knit 2 together) 2 times, knit 2. (6 stitches)
Round 17: Knit.
Round 18: (Knit 2 together) 3 times, working the stitches onto one needle. (3 stitches)
Round 19: Knit.
Bind off.

FINISHING: Stuff the body and the head through the legs. Stuff very firmly. Sew the leg seams, stuffing firmly as you sew. Then sew each arm together and stuff firmly. Attach the arms to the sides of the body and sew to the hips. Embroider the blue eyes and red mouth with French knots. Following the instructions for making trims given in the appendix, and using the large circle as a guide, make four white balls. Sew three balls in place on the body. Attach one ball to the top of the hat and sew the hat to the head. Attach string for hanging.

CLOWN ORNAMENT

MATERIALS: Small amounts of red, white, black and green two-ply knitting yarn, size 3 double-pointed knitting needles (set of four), stuffing material, large-eyed tapestry needle.

Right Leg

DIRECTIONS: Work in rows with two double-pointed knitting needles. With black, cast 12 stitches onto one double-pointed needle.
Row 1: Purl.
Row 2: Knit.
Row 3: Purl 6, (purl 2 together) 2 times, purl 2. (10 stitches)

Row 4: Knit 1, (knit 2 together) 2 times, knit 5. Cut black; attach red. (8 stitches)
Rows 5 and 7: Purl.
Rows 6 and 8: Knit.
Row 9: Purl. Cut red yarn; leave the stitches on the double-pointed needle and set aside to be worked later.

Left Leg

DIRECTIONS: Work in rows with two double-pointed knitting needles. With black, cast 12 stitches onto one double-pointed needle.
Row 1: Purl.
Row 2: Knit.
Row 3: Purl 2, (purl 2 together) 2 times, purl 6. (10 stitches)
Row 4: Knit 5, (knit 2 together) 2 times, knit 1. Cut black; attach red. (8 stitches)
Rows 5 and 7: Purl.
Rows 6 and 8: Knit.
Join legs: Working from the right side, knit across the first 4 stitches of the left leg, which are on the needle. (This will become the first needle.) Knit the remaining 4 stitches of the left leg and the first 4 stitches of the right leg onto the second double-pointed needle; this will become the front of the body. With the third double-pointed needle, knit the remaining 4 stitches of the right leg. Mark this last stitch as the end of the round; this will be the center back of the ornament.

Body

DIRECTIONS: Work in rounds with the four double-pointed knitting needles.

NOTE: Always mark the end of each round by placing a safety pin in the last stitch of the round. Move the pin when you reach this stitch and replace it in the new stitch just formed.

Round 1: Knit. (16 stitches)
Round 2: Knit 1, (knit into the front and the back of the stitch, knit 3) 3 times, knit into the front and the back of the stitch, knit 2. (20 stitches)
Rounds 3, 4, 5, 6, 7, 8, 9 and 10: Knit.
Round 11: Knit 2, knit 2 together, knit 12, knit 2 together, knit 2. (18 stitches)
Rounds 12 and 13: Knit.
Round 14: Knit 2, knit 2 together, knit 10, knit 2 together, knit 2. (16 stitches)
Round 15: Knit around the round, placing 4 stitches on the first needle, 8 stitches on the second needle and 4 stitches on the third needle.
Rounds 16, 17 and 18: Knit.
Round 19: *Knit 2 stitches together.* Repeat from * to * around the round. Cut red; attach white. (8 stitches)

Head

DIRECTIONS: Continue working in rounds with the four double-pointed knitting needles.
Round 1: Knit.
Round 2: *Knit into the front and the back of the

stitch.* Repeat from * to * around the round. (16 stitches)

Round 3: Knit.

Round 4: Knit 1, (knit into the front and the back of the stitch, knit 3) 3 times, knit into the front and the back of the stitch, knit 2. (20 stitches)

Rounds 5, 6 and 7: Knit.

Round 8: Knit 2, knit into the front and the back of the stitch, knit 13, knit into the front and the back of the stitch, knit 3. (22 stitches)

Rounds 9 and 10: Knit.

Round 11: Knit 2, knit 2 together, knit 14, knit 2 together, knit 2. (20 stitches)

Round 12: Knit.

Round 13: *Knit 2 together, knit 3.* Repeat from * to * around the round. (16 stitches)

Round 14: Knit.

Round 15: *Knit 2 together, knit 2.* Repeat from * to * around the round. (12 stitches)

Weaving the head: With the third needle, knit the 3 stitches from the first needle so that there are only two needles, with 6 stitches on each. Place the two needles parallel to each other. Cut the yarn, leaving an end of about 12″ (30.5cm), and thread this end into the large-eyed tapestry needle. *Insert the tapestry needle through the first stitch on the front knitting needle as if to knit and slip the stitch off the knitting needle; insert the tapestry needle through the next stitch on the front needle as if to purl, but leave the stitch on the needle; insert the tapestry needle through the first stitch on the back needle as if to purl and slip the stitch off the knitting needle; insert the tapestry needle through the next stitch on the back needle as if to knit, but leave the stitch on the needle.* Repeat from * to * until all of the stitches have been woven.

Fasten off the yarn.

Arms (make 2)

DIRECTIONS: Work in rows with two double-pointed knitting needles. With white, cast 8 stitches onto one double-pointed needle.

Row 1: Purl.

Row 2: Knit.

Row 3: Purl 2, (purl 2 together) 2 times, purl 2. Cut white; attach red. (6 stitches)

Rows 4, 6, 8, 10 and 12: Knit.

Rows 5, 7, 9, 11 and 13: Purl.

Bind off.

NECK RUFF

DIRECTIONS: Work in rows with two double-pointed knitting needles. With green, cast on 44 stitches.

Row 1: *Knit 1, purl 1.* Repeat from * to * across the row.

Row 2: Knit 1. *Slip 1, knit 1, pass the slip stitch over the knit stitch.* Repeat from * to * to the last 3 stitches. Slip 1, knit 2 together, pass the slip stitch over the knit stitch. (22 stitches)

Row 3: (Knit 1, purl 2 together) 3 times, (knit 1, purl 1) 2 times, (knit 1, purl 2 together) 3 times. (16 stitches)

Bind off.

SLEEVE RUFF (make 2)

DIRECTIONS: Work in rows with two double-pointed knitting needles. With green, cast on 22 stitches.

Row 1: *Knit 1, purl 1.* Repeat from * to * across the row.

Row 2: Knit 1. *Slip 1, knit 1, pass the slip stitch over the knit stitch.* Repeat from * to * to the last 3 stitches. Slip 1, knit 2 together, pass the slip stitch over the knit stitch. (11 stitches)

Row 3: (Knit 1, purl 2 together) 3 times, knit 1, purl 1. (8 stitches)

Bind off.

FINISHING: Stuff the body and the head through the legs. Stuff very firmly. Sew the leg seams, stuffing firmly as you work. Sew each arm together and stuff firmly. Attach the arms to the sides of the body. Place the neck ruff around the neck and join at the back. Repeat for the sleeve ruffs. Following the instructions for making trims given in the appendix, and using the large circle as a guide, make one green ball and one red ball. Sew one green ball to the clown's stomach and one red ball to the top of his head. Using the small circle as a guide, make one red ball; sew in place as a nose. Make hair by working clipped turkey work around the clown's head. Embroider the eyes and mouth. Attach string for hanging.

CHOIR BOY ORNAMENT

MATERIALS: Small amounts of white, pink, black, yellow, blue and red two-ply knitting yarn, size 3 double-pointed knitting needles (set of four), stuffing material, large-eyed tapestry needle, red construction paper, white construction paper.

Legs

DIRECTIONS: Work in rounds with four double-pointed knitting needles. With black, cast 16 stitches onto one double-pointed needle. Divide the stitches onto three needles, placing 4 stitches on the first needle, 8 stitches on the second needle (the front of the body) and 4 stitches on the third needle. Mark the last stitch for the end of the round; this will be the center back of the ornament. Join, being careful not to twist the stitches.

NOTE: Always mark the end of each round by placing a safety pin in the last stitch of the round. Move the pin when you reach this stitch and replace it in the new stitch just formed.

Rounds 1, 2, 3, 4, 5, 6, 7, 8 and 9: Knit.

Round 10: Knit. Cut black; attach white.

Body

DIRECTIONS: Continue knitting in rounds with the four double-pointed needles.
Round 1: Knit 1, (knit into the front and the back of the stitch, knit 3) 3 times, knit into the front and the back of the stitch, knit 2. (20 stitches)
Rounds 2, 3, 4, 5, 6, 7, 8 and 9: Knit.
Round 10: Knit 2, knit 2 together, knit 12, knit 2 together, knit 2. (18 stitches)
Rounds 11 and 12: Knit.
Round 13: Knit 2, knit 2 together, knit 10, knit 2 together, knit 2. (16 stitches)
Rounds 14, 15, 16 and 17: Knit.
Round 18: *Knit 2 together.* Repeat from * to * around the round. Cut white; attach pink. (8 stitches)

Head

DIRECTIONS: Continue working in rounds with the four double-pointed needles.
Round 1: Knit.
Round 2: *Knit into the front and the back of the stitch.* Repeat from * to * around the round. (16 stitches)
Round 3: Knit.
Round 4: Knit 1, (knit into the front and the back of the stitch, knit 3) 3 times, knit into the front and the back of the stitch, knit 2. (20 stitches)
Rounds 5, 6 and 7: Knit.
Round 8: Knit 2, knit into the front and the back of the stitch, knit 13, knit into the front and the back of the stitch, knit 3. (22 stitches)
Rounds 9 and 10: Knit.
Round 11: Knit 2, knit 2 together, knit 14, knit 2 together, knit 2. (20 stitches)
Round 12: Knit.
Round 13: *Knit 2 together, knit 3.* Repeat from * to * around the round. (16 stitches)
Round 14: Knit.
Round 15: *Knit 2 together, knit 2.* Repeat from * to * around the round. (12 stitches)
Weaving the head: With the third needle, knit the 3 stitches from the first needle so that there are only two needles, with 6 stitches on each. Place the two needles parallel to each other. Cut the yarn, leaving an end of about 12" (30.5cm), and thread this end into the large-eyed tapestry needle. *Insert the tapestry needle through the first stitch on the front knitting needle as if to knit and slip the stitch off the knitting needle; insert the tapestry needle through the next stitch on the front needle as if to purl, but leave the stitch on the needle; insert the tapestry needle through the first stitch on the back needle as if to purl and slip the stitch off the knitting needle; insert the tapestry needle through the next stitch on the back needle as if to knit, but leave the stitch on the needle.* Repeat from * to * until all of the stitches have been woven. Fasten off the yarn.

Arms (make 2)

DIRECTIONS: Work in rows with two double-pointed knitting needles. With pink, cast 8 stitches onto one needle.
Row 1: Purl.
Row 2: Knit.
Row 3: Purl 2, (purl 2 together) 2 times, purl 2. Cut pink; attach white. (6 stitches)
Rows 4, 6, 8, 10 and 12: Knit.
Rows 5, 7, 9, 11 and 13: Purl.
Bind off.

COLLAR

DIRECTIONS: Work in rows with two double-pointed needles. With black, cast on 44 stitches.
Row 1: *Knit 1, purl 1.* Repeat from * to * across the row.
Row 2: *Knit 1, purl 1.* Repeat from * to * across the row. Cut black; attach white.
Row 3: Knit 1. *Slip 1, knit 1, pass the slip stitch over the knit stitch.* Repeat from * to * to the last 3 stitches. Slip 1, knit 2 together, pass the slip stitch over the knit stitch. (22 stitches)
Row 4: (Knit 1, purl 2 together) 3 times, (knit 1, purl 1) 2 times, (knit 1, purl 2 together) 3 times. (16 stitches)
Row 5: *Knit 1, purl 1.* Repeat from * to * across the row.
Bind off.

FINISHING: Stuff the body and the head through the bottom. Stuff very firmly. Sew together across the bottom. Sew each arm together, stuffing firmly as you work. Attach the arms to the sides of the body. Place the collar around the neck and join at the back. Make hair by working unclipped turkey work around the choir boy's head. Embroider the eyes and mouth. Make one 1 1/2" x 1 1/4" (3.8cm x 3.2cm) rectangle out of red construction paper, and one 1 1/2" x 1 1/4" (3.8cm x 3.2cm) rectangle out of white construction paper. Paste the white rectangle on the red rectangle and fold in half to make a book. Stitch or glue the book to the choir boy's hands.

ANGEL ORNAMENT

MATERIALS: Small amounts of metallic white, pink, blue and white two-ply knitting yarn, small amount of yellow four-ply knitting worsted, size 3 double-pointed knitting needles (set of four), stuffing material, large-eyed tapestry needle, cardboard, gold or silver foil, pipe cleaner.

Right Leg

DIRECTIONS: Work in rows with two double-pointed knitting needles. With metallic white, cast 12 stitches onto one double-pointed needle.

Row 1: Purl.
Row 2: Knit.
Row 3: Purl 6, (purl 2 together) 2 times, purl 2. (10 stitches)
Row 4: Knit 1, (knit 2 together) 2 times, knit 5. Cut metallic white; attach pink. (8 stitches)
Rows 5 and 7: Purl.
Rows 6 and 8: Knit.
Row 9: Purl. Cut pink yarn, but leave the stitches on the double-pointed needle and set aside to be worked later.

Left Leg

DIRECTIONS: work in rows with two double-pointed knitting needles. With metallic white, cast 12 stitches onto one double-pointed needle.
Row 1: Purl.
Row 2: Knit.
Row 3: Purl 2, (purl 2 together) 2 times, purl 6. (10 stitches)
Row 4: Knit 5, (knit 2 together) 2 times, knit 1. Cut metallic white; attach pink.
Rows 5, 7 and 9: Purl.
Rows 6 and 8: Knit.
Join legs: Working from the right side, knit across the first 4 stitches of the left leg, which are on the needle. (This will become the first needle.) Knit the remaining 4 stitches of the left leg and the first 4 stitches of the right leg onto the second double-pointed needle; this will become the front of the body. With the third double-pointed needle, knit the remaining 4 stitches of the right leg. Mark this last stitch as the end of the round; this will be the center back of the ornament. Cut pink; attach metallic white.

Body

DIRECTIONS: Work in rounds with the four double-pointed knitting needles.

NOTE: Always mark the end of each round by placing a safety pin in the last stitch of the round. Move the pin when you reach this stitch and replace it in the new stitch just formed.

Round 1: Knit. (16 stitches)
Round 2: Knit 1, (knit into the front and the back of the stitch, knit 3) 3 times, knit into the front and the back of the stitch, knit 2. (20 stitches)
Rounds 3, 4, 5, 6, 7, 8, 9 and 10: Knit.
Round 11: Knit 2, knit 2 together, knit 12, knit 2 together, knit 2. (18 stitches)
Rounds 12 and 13: Knit.
Round 14: Knit 2, knit 2 together, knit 10, knit 2 together, knit 2. (16 stitches)
Round 15: Knit around the round, placing 4 stitches on the first needle, 8 stitches on the second needle and 4 stitches on the third needle.
Rounds 16, 17 and 18: Knit.
Round 19: *Knit 2 together.* Repeat from * to * around the round. Cut metallic white; attach pink.

Head

DIRECTIONS: Continue working in rounds with the four double-pointed needles.
Round 1: Knit.
Round 2: *Knit into the front and the back of the stitch.* Repeat from * to * around the round. (16 stitches)
Round 3: Knit.
Round 4: Knit 1, (knit into the front and the back of the stitch, knit 3) 3 times, knit into the front and the back of the stitch, knit 2. (20 stitches)
Rounds 5, 6 and 7: Knit.
Round 8: Knit 2, knit into the front and the back of the stitch, knit 13, knit into the front and the back of the stitch, knit 3. (22 stitches)
Rounds 9 and 10: Knit.
Round 11: Knit 2, knit 2 together, knit 14, knit 2 together, knit 2. (20 stitches)
Round 12: Knit.
Round 13: *Knit 2 together, knit 3.* Repeat from * to * around the round. (16 stitches)
Round 14: Knit.
Round 15: *Knit 2 together, knit 2.* Repeat from * to * around the round. (12 stitches)
Weaving the head: With the third needle, knit the 3 stitches from the first needle so that there are only two needles, with 6 stitches on each. Place the two needles parallel to each other. Cut the yarn, leaving an end of about 12″ (30.5cm), and thread this end into the large-eyed tapestry needle. *Insert the tapestry needle through the first stitch on the front knitting needle as if to knit and slip the stitch off the knitting needle; insert the tapestry needle through the next stitch on the front needle as if to purl, but leave the stitch on the needle; insert the tapestry needle through the first stitch on the back needle as if to purl and slip the stitch off the knitting needle; insert the tapestry needle through the next stitch on the back needle as if to knit, but leave the stitch on the needle.* Repeat from * to * until all of the stitches have been woven. Fasten off the yarn.

Arms (make 2)

DIRECTIONS: Work in rows with two double-pointed knitting needles. With pink, cast 8 stitches onto one needle.
Row 1: Purl.
Row 2: Knit.
Row 3: Purl 2, (purl 2 together) 2 times, purl 2. Cut pink; attach metallic white. (6 stitches)
Rows 4, 6, 8, 10 and 12: Knit.
Rows 5, 7, 9, 11 and 13: Purl.
Bind off.

FINISHING: Stuff the body and the head through the legs. Stuff very firmly. Sew the leg seams, stuffing as you sew. Then sew each arm together and stuff firmly. Attach the arms to the sides of the body. Make a fringe along the bottom of the skirt by working unclipped turkey work.

Embroider the eyes and the mouth. Sew the hands together, if desired.

Hair: Cut fifteen strands of four-ply yellow yarn, each 7″ (18cm) long. Carefully unwind each strand into four curly plies. Place the "curls" on a piece of heavy paper and, with a piece of matching yarn, stitch the curls to the paper, sewing down the middle of the hair. Tear off the paper and center the "wig" on the angel's head. Stitch down the center part and along the hairline with matching yarn. Cut the hair to the desired length.

Halo: Mold a thin pipe cleaner to the proper circular shape. Cover with gold or silver foil and sew or glue in place.

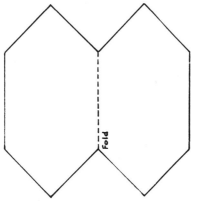

Pattern for Angel Wings

Wings: Although the angel's hair covers her wings, you may wish to attach a pair of wings for the sake of accuracy. Using the pattern for the wings, cut one pair of wings from a lightweight cardboard and two from gold or silver foil. Cover the cardboard with the foil and fold along the fold line. Glue or sew the wings to the angel along the fold line. Attach string for hanging.

SNOWMAN ORNAMENT

MATERIALS: Small amounts of red, white and black two-ply knitting yarn, size 3 double-pointed knitting needles (set of four), stuffing material, large-eyed tapestry needle.

Right Leg

DIRECTIONS: Work in rows with two double-pointed needles. With black, cast 12 stitches onto one double-pointed needle.
Row 1: Purl.
Row 2: Knit.
Row 3: Purl 6, (purl 2 together) 2 times, purl 2. (10 stitches)
Row 4: Knit 1, (knit 2 together) 2 times, knit 5. (8 stitches)
Row 5: Purl. Cut black; attach white.
Rows 6 and 8: Knit.

Row 7: Purl.
Row 9: Purl. Cut white yarn; leave the stitches on the double-pointed needle and set aside to be worked later.

Left Leg

DIRECTIONS: work in rows with two double-pointed knitting needles. With black, cast 12 stitches onto one double-pointed needle.
Row 1: Purl.
Row 2: Knit.
Row 3: Purl 2, (purl 2 together) 2 times, purl 6. (10 stitches)
Row 4: Knit 5, (knit 2 together) 2 times, knit 1. (8 stitches)
Row 5: Purl. Cut black; attach white.
Rows 6 and 8: Knit.
Rows 7 and 9: Purl.
Join legs: Working from the right side, knit across the first 4 stitches of the left leg, which are on the needle. (This will become the first needle.) Knit the remaining 4 stitches of the left leg and the first 4 stitches of the right leg onto the second double-pointed needle; this will become the front of the body. With the third double-pointed needle, knit the remaining 4 stitches of the right leg. Mark this last stitch as the end of the round; this will be the center back of the ornament.

Body

DIRECTIONS: Work in rounds with the four double-pointed needles.

NOTE: Always mark the start of each round by placing a safety pin in the first stitch of the round. Move the pin when you reach this stitch and replace it in the new stitch just formed.

Round 1: Knit. (16 stitches)
Round 2: Knit 1, (knit into the front and the back of the stitch, knit 3) 3 times, knit into the front and the back of the stitch, knit 2. (20 stitches)
Rounds 3, 4, 5, 6, 7, 8, 9 and 10: Knit.
Round 11: Knit 2, knit 2 together, knit 12, knit 2 together, knit 2. (18 stitches)
Rounds 12 and 13: Knit.
Round 14: Knit 2, knit 2 together, knit 10, knit 2 together, knit 2. (16 stitches)
Round 15: Knit around the round, placing 4 stitches on the first needle, 8 stitches on the second needle and 4 stitches on the third needle.
Rounds 16, 17 and 18: Knit.
Round 19: *Knit 2 together.* Repeat from * to * around the round. (8 stitches)

Head

DIRECTIONS: Continue working in rounds with the four double-pointed knitting needles.
Round 1: Knit.
Round 2: *Knit into the front and the back of the stitch.* Repeat from * to * around the round. (16 stitches)

Round 3: Knit.
Round 4: Knit 1, (knit into the front and the back of the stitch, knit 3) 3 times, knit into the front and the back of the stitch, knit 2. (20 stitches)
Rounds 5, 6 and 7: Knit.
Round 8: Knit 2, knit into the front and the back of the stitch, knit 13, knit into the front and the back of the stitch, knit 3. (22 stitches)
Rounds 9 and 10: Knit.
Round 11: Knit 2, knit 2 together, knit 14, knit 2 together, knit 2. (20 stitches)
Round 12: Knit.
Round 13: *Knit 2 together, knit 3.* Repeat from * to * around the round. (16 stitches)
Round 14: Knit.
Round 15: *Knit 2 together, knit 2.* Repeat from * to * around the round. (12 stitches)
Weaving the head: With the third needle, knit the 3 stitches from the first needle so that there are only two needles, with 6 stitches on each. Place the two needles parallel to each other. Cut the yarn, leaving an end of about 12″ (30.5cm), and thread this end into the large-eyed tapestry needle. *Insert the tapestry needle through the first stitch on the front knitting needle as if to knit and slip the stitch off the knitting needle; insert the tapestry needle through the next stitch on the front needle as if to purl, but leave the stitch on the needle; insert the tapestry needle through the first stitch on the back needle as if to purl and slip the stitch off the knitting needle; insert the tapestry needle through the next stitch on the back needle as if to knit, but leave the stitch on the needle.* Repeat from * to * until all of the stitches have been woven. Fasten off the yarn.

HAT

DIRECTIONS: Work in rounds with four double-pointed knitting needles. With black, cast 8 stitches onto one double-pointed knitting needle. Divide the stitches onto three needles; join, being careful not to twist the stitches.

NOTE: Always mark the start of each round by placing a safety pin in the first stitch of the round. Move the pin when you reach this stitch and replace it in the new stitch just formed.

Round 1: Knit.
Round 2: *Knit 1, knit into the front and the back of the stitch.* Repeat from * to * around the round. (12 stitches)
Round 3: Knit.
Round 4: *Knit into the front and the back of the stitch.* Repeat from * to * around the round. (24 stitches)
Round 5: Knit.
Round 6: Purl.
Rounds 7, 8, 9, 10, 11, 12, 13, 14, 15, 16, 17, 18, 19, 20 and 21: Knit.
Bind off.

SCARF

DIRECTIONS: Work in rows with two double-pointed knitting needles. With red, cast on 3 stitches.
Row 1: Knit.
Row 2: Knit.
Repeat these 2 rows until the scarf measures approximately 8″ (20.5cm). Bind off.

FINISHING: Stuff the body and the head through the legs. Stuff very firmly. Sew the leg seams, stuffing firmly as you work. Embroider the eyes, nose, mouth and buttons with large French knots. Attach the hat to the head. If necessary, stuff the hat lightly to make it stand up. Tie the scarf around the snowman's neck. Attach string for hanging.

9.
EDGINGS AND TRIMMINGS

My husband often accuses me of being related to a pack rat—those clever little rodents who hoard strange articles in their nests—because I am forever collecting things that I'm sure I'm going to need someday. "Throw it out," he implores, "you know you'll never use that." Most of the time he's right, but there have been a few occasions when collecting has paid off, figuratively if not literally. I can't help but feel that if an item becomes valuable this year, it will be worth more next year. The occasional clever purchase only encourages me to collect more. Nothing is ever thrown out or sold, and so my collection grows.

I have become, over the years, a constant visitor to what my husband terms "junk shops," those marvelous little stores that sell things that aren't quite antiques, but are still old. One of the things I love to buy is old lace. A piece of old lace might someday turn a perfectly plain dress into an elegant gown. (Usually what happens is that I decide I'm going to use the old lace and then discover I don't have enough to finish the project.)

Lace, of course, is made in various ways, and I can usually identify the method that was used to make it. In one of my favorite shops I once found a small handkerchief trimmed with a lace that I couldn't identify. I, of course, had to buy the handkerchief despite my husband's cries of, "Not that, too!" I studied that piece of lace for a long time before I realized with absolute glee that the lace trimming had been knitted! I immediately felt a kinship with that unknown lady who, like me, had found something else to do with her knitting needles. That small handkerchief stimulated a knitted lace research project. Something told me that my unknown lady hadn't invented knitted lace. Old knitting books bore out my theory; the knitting of lace is a very old craft.

Knitting lace edgings and trimmings can be a lot of fun, and the results can be very useful. You can use edging as shelf trimming, sew lace on a pillow case, make a border for a purchased bedspread, turn a pair of ready-made curtains into a unique window treatment, make a set of plain place mats or a tablecloth into elegant table linen, trim a plain pillow, decorate your Christmas tree, or change that perfectly plain dress into a splendid gown.

In this chapter you will find instructions for nine different lace trimmings. All of the samples were made with a pair of size 4 knitting needles and crochet cotton. You can make the lace more delicate by using smaller-sized needles and a thinner thread like tatting cotton. Bulkier lace calls for larger needles and heavier thread. You may wish to try making some of these edgings with huge needles and bulky yarn for an interesting trimming that would be large enough to use as a canopy for an old-fashioned bed.

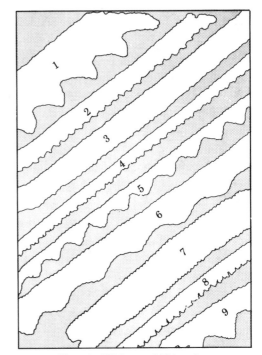

Chart for Edgings and Trimmings

LACE EDGING 1

DIRECTIONS: Cast on 19 stitches.
Row 1: Purl.
Row 2: Knit 1, yarn over, knit 2 together, knit 1, yarn over, knit 2 together, (purl 1, knit 1) 6 times, purl 1.
Row 3: (Knit 1, purl 1) 6 times, knit 1, purl 6.
Row 4: Knit 2, yarn over, knit 2 together, knit 1, yarn over, knit 2 together, (purl 1, knit 1) 5 times, purl 2 together. (18 stitches)
Row 5: (Knit 1, purl 1) 5 times, knit 1, purl 7. (18 stitches)

Knitted Lace as Shelf Trimming

Row 6: Knit 3, yarn over, knit 2 together, knit 1, yarn over, knit 2 together, (purl 1, knit 1) 4 times, purl 2 together. (17 stitches)

Row 7: (Knit 1, purl 1) 4 times, knit 1, purl 8. (17 stitches)

Row 8: Knit 1, yarn over, knit 2 together, knit 1, yarn over, knit 2 together, knit 1, yarn over, knit 2 together, (purl 1, knit 1) 3 times, purl 2 together. (16 stitches)

Row 9: (Knit 1, purl 1) 3 times, knit 1, purl 9. (16 stitches)

Row 10: Knit 2, yarn over, knit 2 together, knit 1, yarn over, knit 2 together, knit 1, yarn over, knit 2 together, (purl 1, knit 1) 2 times, purl 2 together. (15 stitches)

Row 11: (Knit 1, purl 1) 2 times, knit 1, purl 10. (15 stitches)

Row 12: Knit 3, yarn over, knit 2 together, knit 1, yarn over, knit 2 together, knit 1, yarn over, knit 2 together, purl 1, knit 1, purl 2 together. (14 stitches)

Row 13: Knit 1, purl 1, knit 1, purl 11. (14 stitches)

Row 14: Knit 1, (yarn over, knit 2 together, knit 1) 3 times, yarn over, knit 2 together, purl 2 together. (13 stitches)

Row 15: Knit 1, purl 12. (13 stitches)

Row 16: Knit 2, (yarn over, knit 2 together, knit 1) 3 times, yarn over, knit 2 together. (13 stitches)

Row 17: Purl 13.

Row 18: Knit 3, yarn over, knit 2 together, knit 1, yarn over, knit 2 together, knit 1, yarn over, knit 2 together, knit 1, work 7 stitches in the next stitch—*to work 7 stitches in 1 stitch (knit 1, purl 1) 3 times, knit 1 in the same stitch.* (19 stitches)

When a sufficient length has been worked, bind off after row 17.

LACE EDGING 2

DIRECTIONS: Cast on 7 stitches.

Row 1: Slip 1 as if to purl, purl 2, yarn over, purl 2 together, (yarn over) 2 times, purl 2 together. (8 stitches)

Row 2: Yarn over, knit 2, purl 1, knit 2, yarn over, knit 2 together, knit 1. (9 stitches)

Row 3: Slip 1 as if to purl, purl 2, yarn over, purl 2 together, purl 4. (9 stitches)

Row 4: Bind off 2 stitches, knit 4, yarn over, knit 2 together, knit 1. (7 stitches)

Repeat these 4 rows until the piece is the desired length. Bind off.

LACE EDGING 3

DIRECTIONS: Cast on 12 stitches.

Row 1: Yarn over, knit 1, yarn over, knit 2, (knit 2 together) 2 times, knit 2, yarn over, knit 2 together, knit 1. (12 stitches)

Row 2: Purl.

Row 3: Yarn over, knit 3, yarn over, knit 1, (knit 2 together) 2 times, knit 1, yarn over, knit 2 together, knit 1. (12 stitches)

Row 4: Purl.

Row 5: Yarn over, knit 5, yarn over, (knit 2 together) 2 times, yarn over, knit 2 together, knit 1. (12 stitches)

Row 6: Purl.

Row 7: Yarn over, knit 3, knit 2 together, knit 2, yarn over, knit 2 together, yarn over, knit 2 together, knit 1. (12 stitches)

Row 8: Purl.

Repeat these 8 rows until the piece is the desired length. Bind off.

LACE EDGING 4

DIRECTIONS: Cast on 4 stitches.
Row 1: Yarn over, purl 2 together, knit 1, (yarn over) 2 times, knit 1. (6 stitches)
Row 2: Knit 2, purl 1, knit 1, yarn over, purl 2 together. (6 stitches)
Row 3: Yarn over, purl 2 together, knit 4. (6 stitches)
Row 4: Bind off 2 stitches, knit 2, yarn over, purl 2 together. (4 stitches)
Repeat these 4 rows until the piece is the desired length. Bind off.

Knitted Lace as Trimming on a Pillow Case

LACE EDGING 5

DIRECTIONS: Cast on 4 stitches.
Row 1: Yarn over, knit 4. (5 stitches)
Row 2: Slip 1 as if to purl, knit 1, purl 3.
Row 3: Yarn over, knit 1, yarn over, knit 2 together, knit 2. (6 stitches)
Row 4: Slip 1 as if to purl, knit 1, purl 4.
Row 5: Yarn over, knit 1, yarn over, knit 2 together, yarn over, knit 3. (8 stitches)
Row 6: Slip 1 as if to purl, knit 1, purl 6.
Row 7: (Yarn over, knit 2 together) 3 times, knit 2. (8 stitches)
Row 8: Slip 1 as if to purl, knit 1, purl 6.
Row 9: Slip 1 as if to purl, knit 2 together, pass the slip stitch over the knit stitch, yarn over, knit 2 together, yarn over, knit 3. (7 stitches)
Row 10: Slip 1 as if to purl, knit 1, purl 5.
Row 11: Slip 1 as if to purl, knit 2 together, yarn over, knit 2 together, knit 2. (6 stitches)
Row 12: Slip 1 as if to purl, knit 1, purl 4.
Row 13: Slip 1 as if to purl, knit 2 together, pass the slip stitch over the knit stitch, knit 3. (4 stitches)
Row 14: Slip 1 as if to purl, knit 1, purl 2.
Repeat from row 1 until the piece is the desired length. Bind off.

LACE EDGING 6

DIRECTIONS: Cast on 7 stitches.
Row 1: (Yarn over, purl 2 together) 2 times, knit 1, yarn over, knit 2. (8 stitches)
Row 2: Knit 2, purl 4, yarn over, purl 2 together. (8 stitches)
Row 3: (Yarn over, purl 2 together) 3 times, yarn over, knit 2. (9 stitches)
Row 4: Knit 2, purl 5, yarn over, purl 2 together. (9 stitches)
Row 5: (Yarn over, purl 2 together) 3 times, knit 1, yarn over, knit 2. (10 stitches)
Row 6: Knit 2, purl 6, yarn over, purl 2 together. (10 stitches)
Row 7: (Yarn over, purl 2 together) 4 times, yarn over, knit 2. (11 stitches)
Row 8: Knit 2, purl 7, yarn over, purl 2 together. (11 stitches)
Row 9: (Yarn over, purl 2 together) 4 times, knit 1, yarn over, knit 2. (12 stitches)
Row 10: Knit 2, purl 8, yarn over, purl 2 together. (12 stitches)
Row 11: (Yarn over, purl 2 together) 3 times, (purl 2 together) 2 times, yarn over, knit 2. (11 stitches)
Row 12: Knit 2, purl 7, yarn over, purl 2 together. (11 stitches)
Row 13: (Yarn over, purl 2 together) 2 times, knit 1, (purl 2 together) 2 times, yarn over, knit 2. (10 stitches)
Row 14: Knit 2, purl 6, yarn over, purl 2 together. (10 stitches)
Row 15: (Yarn over, purl 2 together) 2 times, (purl 2 together) 2 times, yarn over, knit 2. (9 stitches)
Row 16: Knit 2, purl 5, yarn over, purl 2 together. (9 stitches)
Row 17: Yarn over, purl 2 together, knit 1, (purl 2 together) 2 times, yarn over, knit 2. (8 stitches)
Row 18: Knit 2, purl 4, yarn over, purl 2 together. (8 stitches)
Row 19: Yarn over, (purl 2 together) 3 times, yarn over, knit 2. (7 stitches)
Row 20: Knit 2, purl 3, yarn over, purl 2 together. (7 stitches)
Repeat from row 1 until the piece is the desired length. Bind off.

INSERTION LACE 7

DIRECTIONS: Cast on 12 stitches.
Row 1: Knit 2, yarn over, (knit 2 together) 2 times, (yarn over) 2 times, knit 2 together, knit 2, yarn over, knit 2 together.
Row 2: Knit 2, yarn over, knit 2 together, knit 2, purl 1, knit 3, yarn over, knit 2 together.
Row 3: Knit 2, yarn over, knit 2 together, knit 6, yarn over, knit 2 together.
Row 4: Knit 2, yarn over, knit 2 together, knit 6, yarn over, knit 2 together.
Repeat from row 1 until the piece is the desired length. Bind off. Thread a ribbon through the middle row of eyelets.

LACE EDGING 8

DIRECTIONS: Cast on 6 stitches.
Row 1: Slip 1 as if to purl, knit 2, yarn over, knit 2 together, knit 1.

Row 2: Slip 1 as if to purl, knit 2, yarn over, knit 2 together, knit 1.

Row 3: Slip 1 as if to purl, knit 2, yarn over, knit 2 together, knit 1.

Row 4: Work 6 stitches in the first stitch—*to work 6 stitches in 1 stitch (knit into the front and the back of the stitch) 3 times*—slip each of the first 5 stitches on the right-hand needle over the sixth stitch, knit 2, yarn over, knit 2 together, knit 1.

Repeat from row 1 until the piece is the desired length. Bind off.

LACE EDGING 9

DIRECTIONS: Cast on 7 stitches.

Row 1: Knit 7.

Row 2: Purl 1, yarn over, purl 2 together, purl 1, (yarn over) 2 times, purl 2 together, purl 1. (8 stitches)

Row 3: Knit 3, purl 1, knit 1, yarn over, purl 2 together, purl 1. (8 stitches)

Row 4: Purl 1, yarn over, purl 2 together, purl 5.

Row 5: Knit 5, yarn over, purl 2 together, purl 1.

Row 6: Purl 1, yarn over, purl 2 together, purl 1, (yarn over) 2 times, purl 2 together, (yarn over) 2 times, purl 2 together. (10 stitches)

Row 7: (Knit 2, purl 1) 2 times, knit 1, yarn over, purl 2 together, purl 1. (10 stitches)

Row 8: Purl 1, yarn over, purl 2 together, purl 7.

Row 9: Knit 7, yarn over, purl 2 together, purl 1.

Row 10: Purl 1, yarn over, purl 2 together, purl 1, (yarn over, yarn over, purl 2 together) 3 times. (13 stitches)

Row 11: (Knit 2, purl 1) 3 times, knit 1, yarn over, purl 2 together, purl 1. (13 stitches)

Row 12: Purl 1, yarn over, purl 2 together, purl 10.

Row 13: Knit 10, yarn over, purl 2 together, purl 1. (13 stitches)

Row 14: Purl 1, yarn over, purl 2 together, purl 2, (yarn over, yarn over, purl 2 together) 4 times. (17 stitches)

Row 15: (Knit 2, purl 1) 4 times, knit 2, yarn over, purl 2 together, purl 1. (17 stitches)

Row 16: Purl 1, yarn over, purl 2 together, purl 14. (17 stitches)

Row 17: Bind off 10 stitches, knit 4, yarn over, purl 2 together, purl 1. (7 stitches)

Repeat from row 2 until the piece is the desired length. Bind off.

APPENDIX

HOW TO KNIT

There are two methods of knitting: the English and the continental. In the continental method, the thread is held over the index finger of the left hand and is kept tight by being woven around the fingers of the left hand. As you work, the point of the needle catches the yarn and pulls it through the stitch in one continuous motion. In the English method, the thread is held in the right hand and is looped over the top of the right-hand needle with each stitch. Both methods are correct! There are knitters who insist that one method is better than the other, but I have found that the method you eventually choose to use is usually determined by who originally taught you how to knit. Since Miss Marx taught me the English method, these instructions are based upon that way of knitting.

CASTING ON

I feel that casting on is the only difficult part of knitting. Many would-be knitters are "turned off" because they can't learn to cast on. If you have never knitted before, try to find an experienced knitter to cast on for you until you become more proficient in knitting. Once you understand the principles of how knitting is created, you will find that casting on is actually easy to do.

There are many different methods of casting on, but this is my favorite. Make a slipknot on the yarn several inches from the end. This length varies with the number of stitches to be cast on. A rule of thumb is to allow 1″ for every 3 stitches to be cast on. Place the needle in your right hand and put the slipknot on the needle. (*Step 1*)

Place the short end of the yarn in your left hand, and pass this around the index finger and the thumb, holding the yarn across the palm of your hand. (*Step 2*)

Place the point of the needle under the loop on your thumb and bring the long end of the yarn (the yarn from the ball) forward. Wind the long end of the yarn under and over the point of the needle, drawing it through the loop on the thumb. The newly formed stitch is now on the needle. (*Step 3*)

Tighten the stitch on the needle by pulling the short end of the yarn. Repeat until the required number of stitches have been cast onto the needle. (*Step 4*)

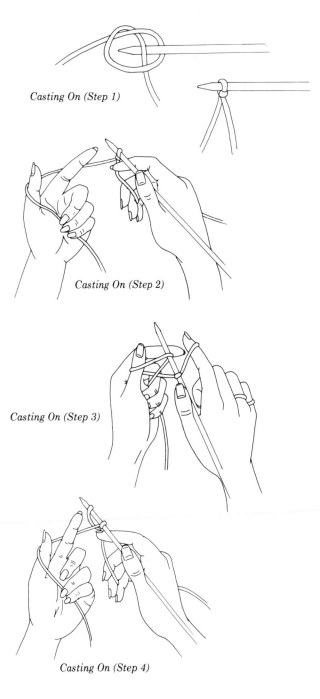

Casting On (Step 1)

Casting On (Step 2)

Casting On (Step 3)

Casting On (Step 4)

Knitting

KNITTING

Hold the needle with the desired number of cast-on stitches in the left hand and hold the empty needle in the right hand. Insert the point of the right-hand needle from the front to the back through the first loop on the left-hand needle. Keep the yarn at the back of the work and pass it under and over the top of the right-hand needle. Draw the loop through the stitch on the left-hand needle. The newly-made stitch is now on the right-hand needle; allow the stitch on the left-hand needle to slip off. Repeat until no stitches remain on the left-hand needle. To work the next row, switch the needle holding the stitches to the left hand and repeat the instructions.

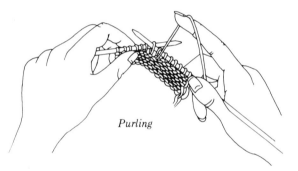

Purling

PURLING

Hold the needles as for knitting, but bring the yarn in front of the needle. Insert the point of the right-hand needle from right to left through the first loop on the left-hand needle. Pass the yarn from right to left over and around the top of the right-hand needle and draw the loop through the stitch on the left-hand needle. The newly-made stitch is now on the right-hand needle; allow the stitch on the left-hand needle to slip off. Repeat until no stitches remain on the left-hand needle. To work the next row, switch the needle holding the stitches to the left hand and repeat the instructions.

KNITTING INTO THE FRONT AND THE BACK OF A STITCH

This is a method of increasing stitches. Knit 1 stitch in the normal way, but do not slip the stitch off the left-hand needle. Knit another stitch through the back of the same stitch and slip the stitch off the left-hand needle. There will now be 1 additional stitch on the right-hand needle.

Knitting 2 together

KNITTING 2 TOGETHER

This is a method of decreasing stitches. Insert the point of the right-hand needle through 2 loops on the left-hand needle. Work these 2 loops as if they were 1 stitch. (To purl 2 together, follow the instructions for purling, but insert the point of the right-hand needle through 2 loops on the left-hand needle.) There will be 1 less stitch on the right-hand needle.

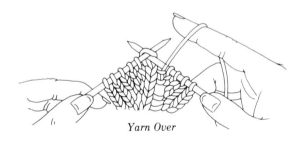

Yarn Over

YARN OVER

In knitting, bring the yarn forward under the needle, then backward over the needle, ready to knit the next stitch. In purling, take the yarn back over the needle and bring it forward ready to purl the next stitch. This will make an extra stitch. Yarn overs are always used to form holes for lace patterns.

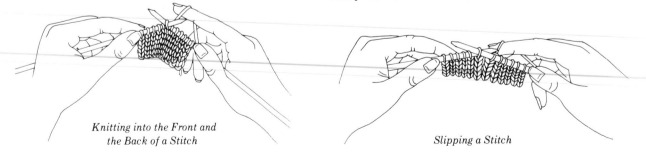

Knitting into the Front and the Back of a Stitch

Slipping a Stitch

SLIPPING A STITCH

Insert the right-hand needle from right to left through the stitch on the left-hand needle and slip the stitch to the right-hand needle without working it. To pass the slip stitch over the knit stitch (a method of decreasing), slip 1 stitch, knit 1 stitch, and then bring the slip stitch over the knit stitch, dropping it off the needle.

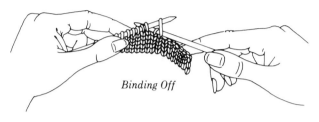

Binding Off

BINDING OFF

Knit 2 stitches. *Slip the first stitch over the second stitch, knit 1.* Repeat from * to * until 1 stitch remains. Cut the yarn and draw it through the last loop. You can also bind off on a purl row by working in the same manner, but purling every stitch instead of knitting.

KNITTING IN THE ROUND

Knitting in rounds, instead of back and forth, will produce either a tubular piece of knitting (such as the plant holders) or a perfectly round piece (such as the round rug or round doilies). Instead of using a pair of straight needles, this knitting is worked on a set of four double-pointed needles and/or a circular needle. These needles come in the same sizes as straight needles but in various lengths. Double-pointed needles come in 7″ (18cm) and 10″ (25.5cm) lengths, and circular needles are available in 16″ (40.5cm), 24″ (61cm), 29″ (73.5cm) and 36″ (91.5cm) lengths.

You always begin working in the center with the double-pointed needles. Cast on the required number of stitches in your usual manner on *one needle only.* Divide the stitches evenly onto three needles and join by inserting the fourth needle into the first stitch. Be extremely careful not to twist the stitches. After you work all of the stitches off a needle, the empty needle is used to work the stitches off the next needle.

You can work any project in the round entirely on the double-pointed needles, but you will find it more comfortable to switch to a circular needle as the stitches are increased. With more than 50 stitches on the double-pointed needles, you may start dropping stitches off the ends of the double-pointed needles. You can begin with a short circular needle and then move on to longer and longer needles as stitches are added. You can work most of the projects in this book, however, on a 24″ (61cm) circular needle.

Since you never reach the point where the needle is free of stitches it is difficult to tell exactly where the round begins. It is therefore very important when knitting in rounds—especially on a circular needle—that you mark the start of each round by placing a marker, such as a safety pin, in the first stitch of each round. Move this marker when you reach this stitch and replace it in the new stitch just formed.

In the beginning you may find that working with the double-pointed needles will be a bit clumsy. But if you keep at it, you'll soon be whipping around the rounds. In the beginning, try to knit with your work lying in your lap or on a table rather than holding the work up in the air as if you were knitting a sweater.

Knitting in the round will always produce stockinette stitch if each round is knitted. To produce garter stitch, you must knit one round and purl one round.

HOW TO WORK WITH MORE THAN ONE COLOR

There are many methods of achieving a multicolored knitted fabric, and a number of them are used in this book. You can knit horizontal stripes, as in the "Ripple Afghan," or you can use the slip stitch technique, as in the bathroom ensemble. These methods are self-explanatory; simply follow the instructions and the color changes will automatically appear. Here, however, are instructions for two more difficult methods of working with more than one color, "stranding" and "bobbin knitting."

STRANDING

When you work a pattern with just two colors, such as the lettering on the "Vegetable Bags," the second color may be carried across the back of the work. This is called "stranding." There are two methods for doing this. Use whichever method is easier for you, but remember that it is extremely important to keep the wool carried across the back at an even tension. The knitting should have the same elasticity as regular stockinette stitch. Do not pull the yarn too tightly, and keep the work loose on the reverse side or the pattern will not emerge. To avoid making holes where one color ends and the new color begins, try bringing the new color from underneath. If you are going to "strand" the thread across more than 6 stitches, it is a good idea to twist the unused color around the working thread every 5 or 6 stitches to keep the tension even.

Method One

Knit the required number of stitches with the background color. Join the stranding color and knit the required number of stitches. Knit the next group of background stitches, leaving a sufficient length of the background thread at the *back* of the work to give elasticity to the fabric. Knit the next group of stitches in the stranding color, leaving a sufficient length of this thread at the back of the knitting. Continue in this manner to the end of the row.

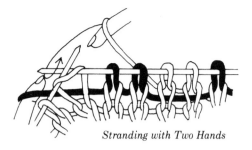

Stranding with Two Hands

Method Two

The diagram shows this method of working with the right hand (the light stitches) while "stranding" with the left hand (the dark stitches). The right hand is ready to make the next stitch, and the left hand is holding the dark thread across the back of the work. While the light stitches are being worked, the left hand keeps the dark thread below and out of the way of the light thread. The procedure is reversed when the dark stitches are worked, and the light stitches must be "stranded" across the back of the work.

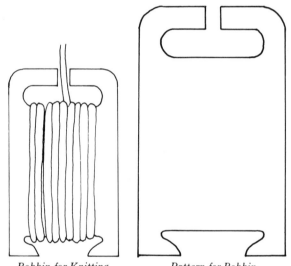

Bobbin for Knitting   *Pattern for Bobbin*

KNITTING WITH BOBBINS

When you work a pattern with many color changes, such as the "Log Cabin Patchwork Quilt," you cannot carry the colors across the back of the work. Not only will you waste a great deal of yarn, but there is always the danger that you will pull the yarn too tightly, which will result in puckered knitting. Instead, you must divide each color into separate units and work with these, twisting one color around the other when you make a change. Rather than having to work with many different balls of yarn, you can use bobbins. These are very easy to work with and will hang at the back of your knitting, eliminating tangles. You can purchase a set of knitting bobbins, or you can make your own. Trace the bobbin pattern on some heavy cardboard and cut out the required number of bobbins. Wind the yarn around the center of the bobbin and pull the working end through the slit.

Working a Knit Row with Bobbins

Keep each bobbin at the back until you are ready to work with it. Knit the last stitch in the old color, and then take this end of the yarn over the new color to be used and drop it. Pick up the new color under this strand and take it over the strand as you begin to work the next stitch with the new color.

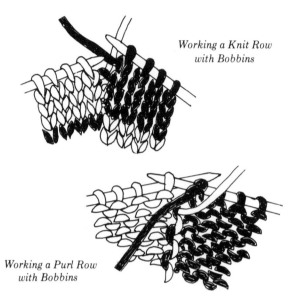

Working a Knit Row with Bobbins

Working a Purl Row with Bobbins

Working a Purl Row with Bobbins

Keep each bobbin at the front until you are ready to work with it. Purl the last stitch in the old color, and then take this end of the yarn over the new color to be used and drop it. Pick up the new color under this strand and take it over the strand as you begin to work the next stitch.

HINTS ON FINISHING

Unlike sweaters or other knitted garments that must be a definite size, most of the projects in this book will require very little finishing. For most of the projects a simple steaming along the ends and side edges to keep the project from curling will be sufficient. To steam a project, lay the work on a padded surface such as an ironing board or even a carpeted floor protected by a large sheet. Dampen a Turkish towel and place it over the knitted project. Hold the iron approximately 4″ (10cm) above the towel and allow the steam to penetrate the towel. *Do not allow the iron to rest directly on the knitting.* Remove the towel and allow the knitting to dry completely before removing it from the padded surface.

WEAVING IN THE ENDS

If the back of a project will show—such as in an afghan—you will want to weave in all of the loose ends of yarn, including the ends left at the start of the cast-on and bind-off rows. For projects where the back will not show—such as pillows—this is optional.

Thread the ends of yarn through a large-eyed tapestry needle and weave the yarn through several stitches on the back of the project. If the ends are too short to thread through the needle, tuck them under the stitches on the back with the point of the needle.

WASHING

If you are a very neat knitter, most of these projects will not need to be washed before they can be used. If, however, your knitting has been carried around in the bottom of your tote bag while you worked on the project, you may find that washing the project before you use it will be required to remove the residue of several half-eaten candy bars. Eventually most of your projects will need to be washed, so it is important that you have some understanding of what is involved.

In general, the method you use for washing any knitted project will depend upon the type of yarn that you have used. A pure wool yarn will require special hand washing in cold water with a special detergent formulated for wool. Acrylic yarn can often be washed in the washing machine and dried in the dryer. Most yarn labels will contain the necessary washing information; so save your labels. *Never wash pieces that have not yet been assembled in the washing machine even if the yarns are machine washable.* If you are not sure how to handle the project, follow these instructions for washing all projects.

Fill a tub large enough to contain your project with cool water and add a gentle soap or special cold water wash. Place the knitting in the solution and allow it to soak for a few minutes. Gently squeeze the suds through the project once or twice but do not rub. Rinse two or three times in clear water, squeezing out the excess water.

After the moisture has been removed, gently lay the piece on a Turkish towel and allow it to dry, away from bright sunlight. Never hang the piece, as most yarn—especially acrylics—will stretch out of shape.

BLOCKING

The term blocking merely means shaping the piece into its final size. Place the article to be blocked right side down on a padded surface, tug it gently into its correct shape and size, and pin evenly around the edges. Always use rustproof pins, placing them approximately 1/2″ (1.3cm) apart. Check to see that all of the stitches and rows run in parallel lines. If the project was washed before blocking, let it dry thoroughly before unpinning. If the project was not washed, steam it lightly with a steam iron or a damp cloth. Hold the iron approximately 4″ (10cm) above the project and allow the steam to penetrate. *Never rest the iron on the knitting.* The edges and the bottoms of all projects will require extra concentrations of steam to keep them from curling. Work slowly making sure that steam has penetrated all areas of the project. Allow the knitting to dry completely before removing the pins.

JOINING PIECES

When joining pieces of a garment to be worn, great care must be taken to use the correct type of seam. Side seams are usually joined with invisible seams, shoulder seams are joined with backstitching, and separate pieces of ribbing or bands that are to be joined to the garment are attached with flat seams. For the projects in this book, however, joinings can be made by whatever method you prefer. In fact, many of the projects—especially the pillows—can be joined by sewing the parts together on the sewing machine, using the same needles and pressure you would use for any knit fabric. Here are instructions for three methods of joining. Whatever method you choose, make sure to pin the seams together first, matching each stitch or row.

Invisible Seam

This will form an invisible seam on the outside and a small ridge on the inside. Place the pieces to be joined side by side with their right sides facing you. Thread a large-eyed tapestry needle with the same yarn used in making the project and weave the yarn into the back of a few stitches. Bring the needle up to the right side at the lower edge of the seam. Pass the needle across to the other side of the work, pick up 1 stitch at the lower edge and draw the yarn through. Pass the needle across the back of the first side, pick up a stitch and draw the yarn through. Continue working in this manner, making rungs and pulling the pieces closer and closer together as you work.

Flat Seam

This will form a flat seam inside and outside. Place the pieces to be joined with the right sides together. Thread a large-eyed tapestry needle with the same yarn used in making the project and weave the yarn into the backs of a few stitches at the lower edge of the seam. Insert the needle through the first stitch at the edge of the back piece and the first stitch at the edge of the front piece and pull the yarn to the front. Now insert the needle through the next stitch at the edge of the front piece and the next stitch at the edge of the back piece and pull the yarn through to the back. Continue working in this manner for the entire seam.

Backstitched Seam

This will produce a very firm seam which will resist stretching. Place the pieces to be joined with the right sides together. Thread a large-eyed tapestry needle with the same yarn used in making the project and weave the yarn into the backs of a few stitches. Bring the needle up from the back of the work through both pieces about 1 stitch in from the seam edge. Beginning at the right edge of the work about 1 stitch in from the edge, pass the needle down through the work 1 stitch to the right, then up through the work 2 stitches to the left. Bring the needle down again 1 stitch to the right and then up through the work 2 stitches to the left. Continue working in this manner for the entire seam. Keep checking the other side of the seam to make sure that you are sewing in a straight line. Make certain that you pull each stitch firmly through the knitting without stretching the pieces being joined or drawing up the stitches too tightly.

FINISHING LACE PROJECTS

No matter how carefully you work, a knitted lace project will need to be washed and blocked for that "professional" look. Use a solution of cool water and a gentle soap or detergent. Gently wash the knitting by squeezing the suds through the project; do not rub. Rinse in clear water until all of the suds have disappeared. Pin the knitting right side down on a flat surface, tugging gently to get the corners square or the shape circular. Be sure that you use rustproof pins or you'll have ugly rust marks. Be sure to shape and pin all loops, scallops, or points along the outside edges. When the knitting is almost dry, steam it lightly with a steam iron. Hold the iron approximately 4″ (10cm) above the project and allow the steam to penetrate. If you do not have a steam iron available, use a dry iron and a damp cloth. *Do not rest the iron on the stitches.* Pay special attention to the edges of the project. When thoroughly dry, remove the pins.

All of the lace projects will look better if they are starched. You can starch the project when you wash it, or use spray starch as you steam the lace.

HOW TO MAKE TRIMS

Adding a special trimming as a finishing touch to a project often means the difference between a project that looks "homemade" and one that has a real professional touch. Here are some trims that you may enjoy making.

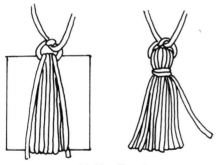

Making Tassels

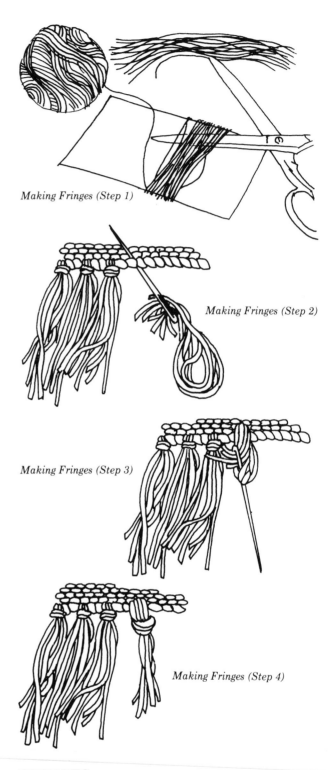

Making Fringes (Step 1)

Making Fringes (Step 2)

Making Fringes (Step 3)

Making Fringes (Step 4)

TASSELS

Wind yarn around a card that is the desired finished length of the tassel. Tie a piece of yarn around the top.

Cut the strands of yarn at the bottom. Tie another piece of yarn around the tassel one-third of the way down from the top.

Attach the tassel to the knitting by tying the yarn at the top.

FRINGES

Wind yarn around a card that is the desired finished length of the fringe. Cut through the strands of yarn along one side of the cardboard. (*Step 1*)

Take four of the strands, double them and thread the cut ends through the eye of a large-eyed tapestry needle. Insert the point of the needle through the edge of the knitted fabric, from the back. (*Step 2*)

Pull the needle out, leaving the loops protruding from under the fabric. Pass the needle through the loops. (*Step 3*)

Remove the needle and pull the loop tightly over the strands of yarn; repeat all along the edge to be fringed. (*Step 4*)

BALLS

Cut two circles out of cardboard. Cut a smaller circle out of the center of each, leaving about 1″ (2.5cm) of the outer circle. Place the two pieces of cardboard together and wind the yarn evenly around and around, through the center hole. (You may change colors, if you desire, for a multicolored ball.) At the start, small balls of the yarn will pass through the center hole. As you near completion, the yarn must be threaded in long lengths on a large-eyed tapestry needle in order to obtain a closely packed circle.

With a very sharp scissors, cut through all of the strands (at the edge) until the cardboard is reached. Pass a piece of string twice around between the cardboards and tie very tightly and securely. Break off the cardboards and trim the yarn ends into a neat, round ball.

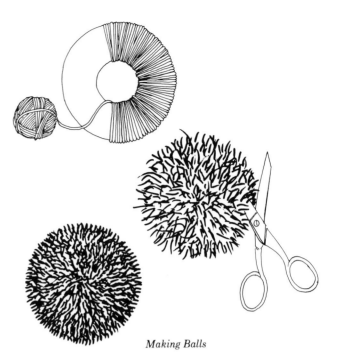

Making Balls

NEEDLE SIZE CONVERSION

The projects in this book call for American-sized knitting needles. Knitters in other parts of the world can make the necessary adjustments by following this chart.

American Knitting Needles	15	13	11	—	—	10 1/2	10	9	8	7
Canadian & British Knitting Needles	000	00	0	1	2	3	4	5	6	7
Metric Knitting Needles (mm)	10	9	8	7 1/2	7	6 1/2	6	5 1/2	5	4 1/2

American Knitting Needles	6	5	3	—	2	1	0	00
Canadian & British Knitting Needles	8	9	10	11	12	13	14	15
Metric Knitting Needles (mm)	4	3 3/4	3 1/4	3	2 3/4	2 1/4	2	1 3/4

INDEX